BLACK
RESILIENCE

The BLUEPRINT
for BLACK TRIUMPH
in the FACE OF RACISM

K. BRAEDEN ANDERSON

Post Hill
PRESS

A POST HILL PRESS BOOK
ISBN: 978-1-63758-507-8
ISBN (eBook): 978-1-63758-508-5

Black Resilience:
The Blueprint for Black Triumph in the Face of Racism
© 2023 by K. Braeden Anderson
All Rights Reserved

Cover design by Cody Corcoran

Post Hill Press
New York • Nashville
posthillpress.com

Published in the United States of America

1 2 3 4 5 6 7 8 9 10

I would like to dedicate the book to my children, and to all of America's Black children across the United States. I love you, and I believe in you. I hope this book makes a difference in your life—whether you read it, or your parents do. No human being or force of nature can stop you from achieving your goals. You are powerful beyond measure or belief. We are Black and resilient.

TABLE OF CONTENTS

INTRODUCTION

PULL UP A CHAIR

IF YOU PICKED UP THIS book, you're probably ready to embark on the journey of self-development and personal success. You already know that, as a person of color, you'll have a different path to those goals than others do. I certainly did. As much as I wish our circumstances were different, I also wish I'd had a book like this when I was starting out in school, in basketball, in law practice, and in life. That's why I wrote it—because I want the path to be smoother for you than it was for me.

I want you to win. I want us to win. I want to share some experiences that I think many of you can relate to. I want to tell you about some strategies that have worked for me, as well as those that didn't. More importantly, though, I want us to embark on a journey together. A journey in self-discovery and self-mastery. A journey toward taking control of our lives and our limitless destinies. A journey toward freedom from oppression and the sting of persecution.

The effects of bias in its various forms and subtypes, including racism, have been and continue to be especially harmful to the Black population. As a Black man in America faced with this reality, I have constantly asked myself, "How do I respond?"

I wrote this book to fill a gaping hole in nonfiction literature on race literature. A multitude of books are aimed at helping white people overcome their own biases, but there is a blatant lack of writing directed at helping the afflicted cope with, adapt to, and succeed within a society in which bias is deeply ingrained. An English professor I interviewed for this book told me, "One of the complaints I'm hearing right now is that there are Black authors being read, but they are Coates, Whitehead, and all the others are slave narratives. This is a real problem that needs addressing." There are others, of course—Brit Bennett, Amanda Gorman—but there's a point there.

Another problem that needs addressing (or more accurately, correcting) is white people explaining Black people to other white people. It's concerning that we have predominantly white educators, authors, and diversity leaders teaching and, for the most part, being the authority on Black experiences, Black problems, and Black solutions.

Instead of a white author preaching to a white audience about Black experiences, this book and its messages are from a Black author talking to a Black audience—you. This is the context in which these conversations should exist.

If you aren't Black and want to participate and engage, you're welcome. We're having a conversation. Come pull up a chair to our table. Pull up a chair if you have the guts. Listen up. Come learn and hear our stories. We'd love to have you join us. This is *our* conversation, though, so we'll do the talking. And this is going to be new for you, but we're not talking to you either. We're talking to each other. This is because it is not white people who have the power to change Black lives. We do, actually. We have control of our success and what happens next. We have the ability to write the next chapter of Black America. The chapter is called Black Resilience. Buckle up.

The overwhelming focus on preventing and eliminating bias makes sense, and don't get me wrong—I have demonstrated a strong commitment to diversity and inclusion initiatives concentrated on reducing and eliminating bias. But waiting and hoping for eventual social change is not a winning strategy. I'm tired of waiting. I'm tired of waiting for white people to treat us equally. I'm tired of asking white people to stop being racist. I'm tired of the endless narratives about Black trauma and victimhood. Aren't you?

The Black community needs immediate relief by way of employing practical tools to overcome bias and succeed while Black, right now. We need proactive strategies designed to help us win in the America of today—to unlock our Black power and excellence, take control of our fate, and chart our own path.

Systemic change with respect to racism and bias has been and will continue to be disturbingly slow, but accepting this discouraging reality is not admitting defeat. Rather, it is the first step to doing something about it. I don't have to tell you that racism is alive and well in America and across the globe and that, unfortunately, the Black community will likely be forced to contend with the impacts of it for many years to come. Understanding this reality raises some proactive questions, such as these:

How do I overcome racism at school and at work?

How can I fight back against unconscious bias?

Can I play offense?

Can I play the game knowing that it's rigged against me and still win?

I wrote this book to answer those questions. I'll share with you some of my own experiences with racism and bias, and I'll reveal the tactics I have used to effectively combat them.

The strategies I will share here are intended to provide you who have been a victim of bias with some tools to achieve some unlikely, shockingly positive outcomes.

THE DICHOTOMY OF INCLUSION

The mainstream approach to battling bias is largely geared toward pressuring white people and large corporations to take performative steps disguised as "confronting biases," as an attempt to eliminate racist tendencies. If it feels like this method is not providing noticeable results, that's because it's not. There's a dichotomy here—the pressure to include versus the reality of what that looks like during recruitment and later, on the job. The diversity and inclusion technique used by public companies is largely aimed at long-term, marginal progress across all visible minority groups. While a noticeable decrease in societal bias one hundred years from now is a virtuous endeavor, it does utterly nothing to help the ambitious Black professional succeed today.

The hiring process has gotten a lot better—especially in large organizations—and we are seeing public companies and global law firms take serious steps to improve their diversity. Yet, despite their improvement and despite their best intentions, recruiting efforts are still falling short.

If the majority of hires year over year come from the same eight Ivy League schools, how can we make progress?

If the same six Black Harvard graduates each receive fifty employment opportunities, does an industry's diversity really improve?

Are these corporations simply waiting for the diversity to improve at Ivy League schools?

Are there not highly talented, highly skilled, Black job candidates at state schools and historically black colleges and universities (HBCUs)?

Despite the fact that, for most companies, there is still a long way to go in terms of recruiting Black talent, in general, things *are* getting better—and more of us are getting in the door. That said, unfortunately, the promotion and retention of Black talent is a different story. Despite our objective merit, we are often perceived as being granted employment opportunities only as a result of a diversity initiative. This perception is of course almost always wrong and almost always racist. But what can we do about it? If our colleagues and superiors perceive us this way, how can we prove ourselves valuable? How do we show others that we are worthy not only of our current position but of a promotion? Getting in the door is only the first step, and while it is not something to overlook, being hired alone is not enough. Once we have penetrated the first gate, we must recognize that our journey is only just beginning. In order to succeed at the company, we must cultivate relationships with people who can help us develop, learn, and grow. Whether it's business, law, or basketball, the ultimate goal is the same: to put together the best team possible. We must work to make sure that those with whom we work respect us and recognize the value we bring. We need strong friendships with our colleagues and mentors in high places. We need sponsors, partnerships, and alliances. We need plans, strategies, and the right skillset.

If you, like me, understand that just getting in the door is not enough, keep reading. There are lots of us who feel this way—those who aspire to identify and take advantage of each and every educational and professional opportunity we encounter. Those of us who want to rise up and challenge the status quo. Those of us who want more than what our white brothers and sisters will freely offer us. Those of us who are willing to fight to achieve what we deserve. This book will show you how to break the shackles that attempt to hold us down and ascend to our rightful place. This book will show you how to win. Just let them try to stop you.

LEARNED HELPLESSNESS

We are not helpless.

First described in 1967 by psychologists J. Bruce Overmier and Martin E. P. Seligman, learned helplessness occurs when repeated exposure to uncontrollable stressors results in individuals failing to use any available control options. It's essentially the "Why try?" question too many of us ask ourselves. We learn to accept that we lack behavioral control over environmental events, which often undermines the motivation to attempt to change our circumstances. Researchers have found a link between this concept of learned helplessness and posttraumatic stress disorder.

Noam Chomsky, a major figure in analytic philosophy and one of the founders of the field of cognitive science, said, "All over the place, from the popular culture to the propaganda system, there is constant pressure to make people feel that they are helpless, that the only role they can have is to ratify decisions and to consume."

That's what learned helplessness does. I know you've seen it, and I know you've felt it, but just because you know the terrain doesn't mean you have to live there. The intervention starts with self-confidence and total rejection of helplessness.

To escape learned helplessness and that feeling that you cannot affect meaningful change in your life, you need a new kind of confidence. Right now, we see a confidence in our race that is reactive, retaliatory. That's counterpunch confidence. I'm suggesting finding a cerebral confidence, resulting from a plan to transcend the obstacles in your path. I wrote this book to address how to take that step from anger, pain, and learned helplessness to inner peace.

BIAS

Even the best of the white community views us with pity, something we'll look at later. That's not the way we want to or should be seen. There are lots of things you can do other than participate in the pity party, and that's what this book represents.

Bias is a big topic, too big to adequately tackle in its entirety in this book. However, if we are to effectively address the intricacies of how race-related bias thwarts attempts to succeed by people of color and create a game plan for how to overcome it, we must understand that racism is simply one of many forms of bias.

Whether conscious or unconscious, bias is a naturally occurring phenomenon and will be forever relevant. As a six-foot-eight Black man covered in tattoos, I know it all too well. An elementary and middle school student who grew up in rural Alberta, Canada, I also know what it feels like to be the only Black child in a town's entire school system. I'm sure you've had similar experiences. Regardless of where you grew up, the issue is the same.

You probably know as well as I do what it's like to have white educators think you're not smart enough to bother teaching or pay any attention to. As a child, you can't put an educator's bias into the proper perspective. They are adults, and most of us were taught to respect and believe our elders. At that young age, we do not yet understand that our teacher is wrong for viewing us and treating us differently. We do not notice the lack of reasoning behind our mistreatment. Most often, Black children respond to this abuse by internalizing it and eventually accepting that they must not be that smart.

They utter statements like, "School is not for me." Or "I'm street smart, not book smart." We use a lot of "my thing" substitutes to hide the pain of what feels like failure. "Sports are my thing." "Rap is my thing." "Drums are my thing." These statements are often prefaced or followed by, "School's not my thing." No one's there to show us that we can have sports and rapping and drums *and* school.

A lot of people in our Black community feel ostracized from white America, and of course, they're going to associate white America with the education system. Educators are not only the ambassadors for white

America, but they are the gatekeepers. They decide who is worthy of white America's acceptance and attention.

I found it extremely challenging to succeed under these conditions, and for much of my life, my grades and general academic performance were a reflection of that. The repugnance of their actions aside, my teachers genuinely believed they were correct about me. They perceived me as a menacing troublemaker, a surefire future criminal, and as a result, they overreacted to my immature behavior and doled out punishments in a manner that reflected the same.

Even then, I could see that had I been white, their perception of me would have been very different. A white kid who talked back to a teacher often got away without even a warning. If I talked back at all, I was sent to the office.

If you don't understand something, it's harder for you to learn, and I didn't feel my teachers put in any effort to help me understand. They looked at me as almost a lost cause and may well have perceived attempting to educate me as a waste of time. There are a lot of factors that may influence how an educator perceives or treats a student. I'm not anti-teacher—I frequently teach business law at Monroe College in the Bronx. Still, I understand burnout and bias. It's not an easy job. You can't be perfect, and you can't help everybody. Regardless of your intentions, you will encounter students in every class with whom you just don't connect. For whatever reason, these students are the other. I was the other. Maybe, for whatever reason, you were too.

My childhood educators and coaches were wrong about me and would likely fall off their chairs today if they learned what I later accomplished. Contrary to what they thought, I *was* smart. School *was* for me. And I *was* worthy of their attention. I became an All-American and All-Canadian high school basketball player, I received more than twenty-five full-ride athletic scholarship offers, I graduated from high school with honors, I played for Canada's national basketball team, I graduated from college in only three years, I made history as the only active NCAA Division 1 basketball player to attend law school while playing, I passed the New York State Bar Exam in one attempt and became a licensed attorney, I landed a job at one of the largest, oldest, and most prestigious law firms on the planet, and my story continues.

People generally tend to view bias (and racism) as a malicious, deliberate decision. Yes, people should stop being racist—wouldn't that be nice? Unfortunately, as we have seen while living through and observing the last century of race relations in America, this solution is not so simple. Yet, of course it makes sense to try; most of the world's largest companies have implemented diversity and inclusion initiatives over the past twenty years. These programs have largely focused on making people aware of their own biases, such as racism or sexism. The goal, of course, is that this awareness will enable people to eliminate their biases or at least take steps toward mitigating them. The unfortunate reality is that these initiatives have been and will continue to be painfully futile and embarrassingly ineffective for all of us, especially those of us who can be categorized by the color of our skin.

These methods fail because, in reality, trying to avoid implicit stereotyping naturally causes people to inappropriately project their biases. People respond by either overcompensating or attempting to suppress their biased thoughts. If I ask you to try not to think of a gray dog or a red car, you will almost certainly think of a gray dog or a red car. If I ask you to try to ignore that the job candidate you are interviewing is a Black female, you will almost certainly focus on nothing else.

Scientific research indicates that human beings instinctively perceive anyone different from us as a threat due to the brain's evolutionary requirement to do so. David Amodio, a professor of psychology and neural science at New York University, wrote, "The capacity to discern 'us' from 'them' is fundamental in the human brain." The fact is that bias is usually a natural and unintentional predisposition.

In order to overcome bias—and succeed today—aspiring Black professionals and business leaders like us will need to be prepared to set anger aside and commit to the process of developing a proactive game plan rooted in empathy, kindness, tact, and thoughtful dialogue. I cannot promise you that this process will be easy, and in fact it may be very difficult, but I can promise you that it will work.

I also know that, for you to hear me, I have to prove myself, and in the next chapter, I'm going to share more experiences that helped shape me and led me to the strategies that allowed me to succeed despite a childhood steeped in racism and physical abuse. It's true that we are required to have different skills and strategies than our white counterparts to achieve success. There's no getting around that. But I'm here to tell you that we are not inadequate. We are powerful beyond measure or belief. No one can stop us.

CHAPTER 1

THE POWER OF BLACK RESILIENCE

IN A *WASHINGTON POST* ARTICLE following the January 6, 2021 insurgence, Cori Bush, a Democrat representing Missouri's First Congressional District in the House of Representatives, wrote about being sprayed with mace when protesting at the police station during the summer of 2021, in Florissant, Missouri, where a police officer had run over a Black man with his car. Representative Bush then compared that to being on the second floor of the Capitol in January 2021 and looking out the windows as she watched Trump and Confederate flags move closer.

"Once I was in my office, and we secured the door, I felt a different kind of burn," she writes. "This time, inside." Later in the article, she asks the question my friends and I asked ourselves that day: "Would this have happened if the rioters were there to fight for Black lives rather than white supremacy? We've been tear-gassed for much less, beaten for much less, and shot for much less. We've been assaulted by law enforcement for much less."

We all know the answer to that one, and we also know how we feel when even the most well-meaning of our white brothers and sisters say that what happened on January 6, 2021 was not America.

I concur with Rep. Bush when she says, "They are wrong. This is the America that Black people know."

Before we go any further, let's be honest. We Black people are angry, annoyed, and exhausted. Racism, which was built into the very foundation of our society, has influenced the creation of U.S. traditions, laws, pol-itics, institutions, behaviors, and social relations.

Being able to look in a mirror and say, "It is I who is going to change. It is I who is going to adapt and adjust" may seem unfair. Yet, if you are going to overcome any obstacle, especially ones as daunting as racism and Black persecution, you are going to have to go through the steps. That begins with taking inventory of what the variables are. You then come up with a strategy for how you're going to approach those variables.

Many Blacks don't believe we can change our lives. Again, that's learned helplessness based on a pattern of treatment and circumstances over hundreds of years. Thanks to learned helplessness, you have a sneaking suspicion that all the strategies and solutions in this book could not possibly work. They sound good enough, but you've heard good before. *We don't have the power*, you might think. *White people have control. We have to teach white people not to hurt us, not to shoot us and kill us, not to ignore us in the classroom.* I reject all these notions, and you should too—because they are not valid. Power does reside in you, and there are a number of variables you can control.

Trust me, I get it. And of course, it is perfectly okay to feel that way. We are allowed to—and we should. After all, there is an awful lot to be pissed about. As a Black person in America, I understand that there are endless reasons to be angry. Here are a few:

I detest how popular culture is still riddled with rampant depictions of racial stereotypes. Representational racism in images permeates our culture, promoting an array of racist ideologies that imply Black inferiority, stupidity, and untrustworthiness.

I am tired of dominant ideological world views and belief systems still normalizing racism. Studies have shown that the majority of Americans continue to believe white people are more intelligent than and generally superior to Black people. These deeply ingrained ideas supported the founding of the United States and the dominance of European colonial empires for centuries through the unlawful acquisition of property, persons, and assets around the world.

I am saddened to know that racial slurs and hate speech are still being used to promote and perpetuate ethnic hierarchies. Racialized code words, like "ghetto," "thug," or "gangster" continue to spread and normalize racist ideas.

I am frustrated that we still have to deal with interactional racism on a daily basis. Hate crimes, false police reports, and police brutality still overtly plague our streets and communities. Police officers murder our brothers and sisters in broad daylight, with no retribution in sight. Every single day, blatant discrimination causes our people to suffer extreme stress, anxiety, and physical harm. How many more brothers and sisters have to die? How many more times? How many more mothers and fathers have to grieve the loss of a loved one?

It is gravely discouraging that institutional and structural racism still prevail. The fabric of our nation's criminal justice system is woven and laced with racist fibers. Decades-long policing policies like "The War on Drugs" and "Stop-N-Frisk" continue to sustain racial gaps in wealth, education, and social status while they preserve white privilege. The slow creep of gentrification persists, resulting in the recurrent displacement of families from Black neighborhoods.

I find it truly despicable that Black Americans still continue to be murdered by police officers. I am exhausted by the unrelenting stream of gut-wrenching news. George Floyd being restrained and knelt on by police in Minneapolis, resulting in his murder, coupled with the unjust killings of Ahmaud Arbery, Breonna Taylor, and other Black Americans, have led to thousands of largely peaceful demonstrations across the nation. Yet tens of thousands of protestors have been assaulted, blackballed, called un-American, arrested, and even killed. Racism is so fundamentally American that when you protest it, people think you are protesting America itself. But what is more American than fighting for social justice? What year is it again? Why is protesting the death of George Floyd a political issue? Why won't racism get any better? Will Black Americans ever be treated fairly?

I just wish Jacob Blake would have let those women fight that day. I just wish Ahmaud Arbery had run a different route that day. I just wish Breonna Taylor and her boyfriend were away on a nice vacation that day. I just wish George Floyd had used a credit card that day. I just wish America valued Black lives. My experience growing up in Okotoks was different and unique in some ways, but unfortunately, I suspect many of my stories will sound all too familiar. When compared to America, Canada's reputation for race relations problems is less severe. Slavery is less historically significant to Canada's identity. In practice, that fact was meaningless to me, and I still suffered rampant mistreatment by Canadian white people throughout my youth.

According to recent U.S. Census Bureau data, Black people make up about 13 percent of the American population. According to recent census data from Statistics Canada, Black people make up only about 3.5 percent of the Canadian population. In Okotoks, Alberta, where I grew up, roughly 0.0085 percent of the population is Black.

Being a minority is a challenging experience in either country. It definitely has been for me, but perspective is everything. Dealing with racism in Canada before moving to America when I was sixteen offered me a learning experience that has since shaped my worldview on these issues. At the time, however, I was forced to grapple with a range of emotions: fear, confusion, anger, and sadness—a lonely experience for a young man with no Black role models to turn to for guidance. Because of the lack of population diversity in my hometown, I had no Black allies and no Black community. In sixteen years,

I never saw a single Black teacher, doctor, dentist, lawyer, or other professional. When I was called racial slurs and mistreated, I had nobody to stand up for me. I had nobody with whom to share my pain and anger. I had no one to turn to for support. No one understood, and no one cared. It was only me, and I was under constant pressure to be a model representative for the Black race.

At age five, I left my lunch at home. When my mother dropped in on my class to hand it to me, she entered the room and saw kids in different stations, engaged in various activities. Some played with blocks. Others were drawing, counting, or playing games. I wasn't at any of the stations. My mom found me sitting glumly in the corner with my head down, playing with chalkboard erasers.

She looked at my teacher, Mrs. Klingbeil, with skepticism and asked the obvious question.

"Why is my son sitting in the corner playing with erasers? Is he in trouble?"

"Oh, he's not in trouble," the teacher replied. "The children are doing stations right now, and he's supposed to be practicing letter sounds."

My mom asked again, "So, why is he sitting in the corner? How long has he been sitting there?"

In response, Mrs. Klingbeil shrugged and said, "Well, I told him to go to the station. I guess he wasn't listening."

"You're treating him differently. Why is that?"

She didn't get an answer. My mom had assumed I would be treated the same as everybody else. She had believed that, and this experience shocked and disappointed her in a profound way. My white mother had believed that her half-black son could be treated like a whole person.

At age six, I was shopping with my mom at a comic bookstore. When we exited the store, I was still happily carrying a pack of Spider-Man game cards for which we had not paid. When my mother realized this, we immediately returned to the store to return the cards. She had me apologize to the store owner for accidentally leaving with them, expecting to receive a similarly understanding reaction as she had received when something similar had happened to her as a young child. Instead, the owner looked at me with utter disgust and proceeded to call the police on a six-year-old. I didn't understand what was happening, didn't really even understand the concept of paying for something. I remember only the anxiety and being hated. I knew I'd done something very bad and that I must be deserving of punishment.

At age seven, I went to the mall with my mom to pick out a "cool" poster for my wall. I was excited to decorate my new bedroom, and she said I could pick out any poster I wanted. When we arrived at the store, I saw

poster designs featuring pirates, firefighters, police officers, and superheroes. I turned to my mom, crestfallen.

"What's wrong?" she asked.

"None of these are for me. All of these guys are white.
I'm Black, Mom."

At age eight, I came inside after recess to discover
that the words "I hate Niggers" had been written on my
lunchbox in sharpie marker.

At age nine, I routinely played street hockey in the
parking lot behind our condo. I aspired to play ice hockey
one day, but my parents could not afford to pay for the
expensive equipment and travel. But in the streets, I was
a strong goal scorer, and my team seldom lost.

One day, after I'd scored a game-winning goal, my
friend Cory said, "Black people don't play hockey. Black
people play basketball." The comment did not bother
me right away, but when I got home, I looked at my walls
with fresh eyes and saw that they were covered with
posters of Wayne Gretzky, Joe Sakic, Mario Lemieux,
and Peter Forsberg. *Cory was right*, I thought. None of
them were Black. I slowly took the posters down, and I
didn't play much street hockey after that.

At age nine, I was playing outside during recess when
a random older boy ran past me and yelled, "I'd like to
buy a nigger." I didn't know what to say when people
said things like this. I was a football and basketball star,

and I had social status and friends. Yelling back with expletives or threats only got *me* in trouble. Sometimes I'd fight the person. That got me in trouble too. The white authority figures around me didn't see things the same way I did. They did not believe calling me those names justified my reactions. So, I eventually learned it was in my best interest to pick and choose my battles. This often meant giving people a pass and making sure assholes knew they couldn't hurt or get a rise out of me.

Cub Scout leaders, even church leaders, and peers called me those names. My nickname throughout my school career was Big Nig. There was nothing I could do about it. This was not something that you could dispute.

At age ten, I got in trouble for interrupting my teacher, Mr. Talbot.

"Go to the office," he ordered.

"I'm sorry," I said. "Please don't kick me out. I'll be quiet, I promise."

Mr. Talbot marched over to the phone beside the door and called the principal's office. "Somebody come get this Negro out of my class," he said.

I was escorted to the principal's office and given detention.

At age ten, I was having a water gun fight with a friend in his front yard.

A police car pulled up, and an officer shouted, "Get down! On the ground now! Drop your fucking weapon!"

Confused, my friend and I both dropped our water guns.

As the police officer approached, he said, "Hey, you better be careful playing with guns. You look like a criminal. I could have shot you."

At age thirteen, as an indentured member of the Mormon Church or, as it is formally known, the Church of Jesus Christ of Latter Day Saints, I went to gospel study (known as seminary) every morning with my cousins. One morning in late October, many kids were wearing Halloween costumes for school dress-up day. When I arrived, we sat on the couches near the door. This was where the cool kids hung out and talked after class. I noticed that Kyle Campbell, who was about three years older than I, was wearing a single white glove, an afro wig, and dark face paint. Kyle's costume was a smashing hit and garnered a steady stream of applause and laughter. He was, of course, as he put it, "Nigga Michael Jackson."

As is the case in many similar situations, it was so scarily normal that, until it was put into context for me, I didn't have the luxury of being offended. When a popular guy two or three years older than you decides to dress up in blackface for Halloween, when everyone else is laughing and you feel outnumbered, you think, "Well, I guess he can do this. It must be OK." Am I alone responsible for stopping him?

At age sixteen, I was on lunch break, playing a game on the computer while a classmate tried to watch over my shoulder.

"Hey," he said. "Which character are you?"

"I'm the Black guy."

An awkward silence was followed by, "You shouldn't say that."

"Shouldn't say what?" I asked.

"That's wrong," he insisted. "You shouldn't say someone is Black."

"What are you talking about?" I asked incredulously.

"You should say African American."

A few minutes later when the teacher returned to the classroom, this student reported me, and the teacher said, "Braeden, apologize for what you said."

"What do you mean?" I demanded. "It's okay to say someone is Black."

"Well," the teacher said, "you made him feel very uncomfortable."

I was forced to apologize to the white boy in my class for making him feel uneasy about my use of the term "Black."

At age seventeen, I was flying to a basketball tournament in Minneapolis and had been graciously given the exit row seat to accommodate my long legs. Exhausted, I immediately closed my eyes and settled in for the long flight.

Before takeoff, an older white-haired flight attendant kicked my leg and said angrily, "Wake up and move to a different seat. No sleeping in an exit row."

I explained that I was just closing my eyes and respectfully refused to give up my seat. Moments later, and with no warning, he had a federal marshal escort me off the plane.

At age twenty-one, I was back in Canada visiting friends and family when I ran into Mark Campbell, the father of Kyle Campbell, who had delighted the crowd at the Halloween party with his "Nigga Michael Jackson" getup all those years earlier. I was with my cousin Kyle Guenard at the time, who is white, and his parents were close with the Campbell family, so we felt compelled to stop and chat for a moment. My cousin and Mark exchanged pleasantries while I stared off into space and counted the seconds until I could respectfully walk away. This worked for a while, but eventually, Mark's attention turned to me.

"I heard you were in a bad car accident," he said.

"Yes," I replied.

"I'm guessing you were driving like a maniac. Did you learn your lesson?"

I exhaled sharply and then summoned the patience to say, "Actually, Mark, I wasn't driving. And it was a drunk driver who hit us. Thanks, though."

At age twenty-two, I interned for a federal judge for a summer in between my first and second year of law school in New Jersey. I worked primarily under the judge's law clerk, who didn't seem to like me very much. During my first week on the job, she told me I looked "more like a basketball player than a lawyer" and that I was "not fooling anybody" by using "big words."

Aside from her weird comments, I did not receive any helpful feedback from her the entire summer. At the end of the summer, she implored the judge not to hire me and wrote an email to administrators at the law school complaining about my poor work product and general lack of professionalism. The judge declined to interview me for the clerkship position.

Although I have certainly experienced bias during my time in the United States, my time spent in Canada was worse. I responded very poorly to Canada's demographic environment. Canadians loved to call me the N-word without repercussions. I suspect that, for some kids, making me mad became an amusing game. This caused me a great deal of pain, not only because the word is harmful but because as the only Black kid in every room, class, or playground, I always felt totally responsible for addressing the situation somehow.

"No. You can't just say that and get away with it. Fuck no."

This got me into a fair bit of trouble.

It's genuinely haunting to consider where I would be in life had I not escaped Canada. I hope you will empathize with my feelings of gratefulness that I am now able to live in America, despite its imperfections, because it is home to an unbreakable and strong Black population. When I moved to North Carolina at sixteen, I saw more Black people in the first twenty-four hours than I had seen in the rest of my life combined. The experience ultimately brought me to tears of joy, helped me find my identity, and emboldened my Black pride. The astronomical increase in Black representation alone made me feel like I could do anything, achieve any goal, and eviscerate any enemy.

However, I soon discovered that finding acceptance within the Black community would present challenges for me, too. Genetically, I am half white and half Black. My mother is Irish Canadian, and my father is Nigerian. I have been labeled "white" by Black friends, and "Black" by white friends. Too white to be Black, and too Black to be white, I often felt that I did not belong anywhere at all.

According to research by Arnold K. Ho, Nour Kteily, and J. M. Chen of the Kellogg School of Management at Northwestern University, white people tend to view biracial people as belonging to the racial category of their non-white parent. Labeling a Black and white person as only Black helps to maintain traditional ideological hierarchies between the two races. This perception of biracial people stems from a history of racist laws that were founded upon the principle referred to as the "one-drop rule." This hypodescent rule determined that any amount, even "one drop," of Black blood rendered a person Black, meaning that the individual was forbidden to classify themselves as white. This research explains that this classification tendency is strongly associated with anti-egalitarianistic belief systems—that is, belief systems that hold that certain racial or ethnic groups are somehow better than others. Black people also generally view Black and white biracial people as being more Black than white, which was strongly associated with more egalitarian views on race. So, the conclusion is the same, but the fundamental reasoning behind each group is in direct opposition. This research also suggests that Black people who hold egalitarian views on race recognize a greater sense of shared discrimination. Perceptions about whether biracial people were discriminated against is highly correlated with the Black community's perception of their Blackness.

"You're Black? Prove it. Tell me your pain. Show me your struggle." Feelings of a shared fate unite us, and suspicions that biracial people have an easy life divide us.

When my mother dropped me off at school, kids would ask, "Were you adopted?" When I went to the barber shop in Canada, they turned me away because they didn't do "Black hair." I grew up listening to Nas, Jay-Z, Kendrick Lamar, Dr. Dre, Tupac Shakur, The Notorious B.I.G., and Wu-Tang Clan. I grew up idolizing Kobe Bryant, Michael Jordan, Oprah Winfrey, Serena Williams, Will Smith, and Denzel Washington. I grew up inspired by the stories of Harriet Tubman, Duke Ellington, Oseola McCarty, Sojourner Truth, Jesse Owens, Phillis Wheatley, Maya Angelou, Martin Luther King, Jr., Malcolm X, and Charles Hamilton Houston. I have dark curly hair, I rocked an Afro in high school, and I played basketball in college.

Is that Black enough for you? Is this what Blackness is? For much of my life, I have lived in an impossible racial gray area. I have not always felt comfortable around a group of all white people, and I have not always felt comfortable around a group of all Black people. Neither group has always made me feel wanted as an ally. My journey toward finding my racial identity has led me to finding an enlightened perception of what race means and what it does not.

Your Blackness is defined by you and no one else— and so is mine. I am who I say I am. I am who I want to be. I am who I feel like I am. I am who I am. I am a proud

Black man. And I vow never to judge the Blackness of others based on the darkness of their complexion. My Blackness is not a plague or a curse, and neither is yours. Our Blackness is not pain. Our Blackness is a gift.

Present circumstances will not dictate what we are capable of. While we may endure struggles that are beyond our control, I know that struggle breeds strength of character. Unbreakable character. Our Blackness is power. There is no earthly being or phenomenon that can stop us. We have been through too much. Just try to stop us.

I believe in the promotion of Black interests, Black ideas, Black businesses, and Black art. I believe that regardless of the color of my skin or yours, we have the power to choose our own destiny. I believe in Black pride and Black self-defense against racial oppression. I believe we have the power to create and build our own versions of the future. Just try to stop us.

BLACK RESILIENCE

In his 1951 poem "Harlem," Langston Hughes speculates, "What happens to a dream deferred?" He asks if it will dry up like a raisin in the sun or if it will just explode, perhaps recalling the Harlem riots of 1935 and 1943, but maybe speaking, in a general sense, about what happens when Black dreams are not only deferred but denied. I submit to you this: these dreams deferred can never be denied and are only temporarily deferred. Temporarily deferred for the last time.

The fulfillment of my dreams are overdue, and I hereby demand them. My dream of a united and equal America. My dream of fair treatment and economic opportunity for my family. In pursuit of these dreams, I have suffered, as have you. I have experienced loss, defeat, and embarrassment, as have you. Yet my suffering does not define me. My dreams are overdue, and I demand them.

Your dreams are overdue, and you must demand them. Your dream of a united and equal America. Your dream of fair treatment and economic opportunity for your family.

Our dreams are overdue, and we must demand them. Our Black ancestors, Black trailblazers, and Black architects of American democracy did as much to contribute to the founding of this great nation as any white man. This nation was founded on their backs, their hopes, their tears, and their dreams. They were beaten, whipped, and bruised. They were killed, raped, sold, humiliated, and tortured. Yet their suffering does not define our destiny. Their dreams make the attainment of ours possible. Our dreams are overdue, and we must demand them.

Our shared pain does not unite us; our shared resilience does. It does not matter what shade of Blackness you bear; you are my family—and we are united in our purpose. Embark on this journey with me. Let's redefine what Blackness means to the world. Let's empower each other and move steadily toward the goals we seek to conquer.

CHAPTER 2

THE WHITE DIVIDE

THERE IS STILL A DEEP disconnect on the topic of racism. Perhaps for the "wokest" whites among us, the problem appears to be getting a *little* better. But unfortunately, for far too many, the understanding gap is widening even more. Black and white Americans are being strategically divided and alienated by polarizing political figures. We are being asked to choose sides, and neither side is listening. A dangerous lack of empathy permeates our culture.

Can we be heard without our experiences being dismissed or invalidated? We are now, more than ever before, simply asking white people to listen. But for many, the concept of white privilege is still too difficult to fully grasp. Many white people do not believe that racial inequality is still a problem in this country because they are not faced with it in their everyday lives, and they cannot summon empathy for those who are suffering. All too often, when we do get their attention, white guilt breeds contempt and defensiveness.

White people sit in implicit bias training dazed and confused, offended, or thinking, *That's not me. This doesn't apply to me.* When they are confronted with the reality of their unintentional, yet pervasive, racist attitudes, a common white reaction is a mix of frustration, denial, and hostility. None of these outcomes is especially helpful or likely to inspire change. All over the country, seasoned experts and staggering budgets are being deployed with abandon to conquer racism in the workplace and rid the world of implicit bias. But the process isn't working well.

Diversity education and implicit bias training programs are designed to expose and remedy the inherently racist assumptions and behavioral patterns that white people display as a result of being raised in a systemically racist society. Forcing individuals to confront this cold reality and understand that they contribute to its perpetuation leads to predictable outcomes. Negative ones. The paradox of human behavior is that while natural selection and other evolutionary forces have enabled us to experience feelings of sympathy and compassion, these same phenomena have also made us sensitive and easily offended.

Our ability to harbor and express both feelings of kindness and hostility have led human beings to become the exceedingly successful social species that we are today. This is because displaying kindness allows us to increase our network and win over new friends, while our potential for hostility prevents us from being taken advantage of.

We humans are complicated. Your coworker who made a marginally racist comment last week probably did not intend to offend you and probably does not hate Black people. Your coworker's behavior was a microaggression: a routine, ordinary, and unconscious act of indignity.

Dealing with and overcoming microaggressions is an art, not a science. The popular, expert-recommended first step is to make the true impact of the person's behavior visible to them in some way: "That was offensive to me because X." On a surface level, this makes sense because, more often than not, the sixty-five-year-old white guy who offended you is totally unaware of the impact of what he said. But does "educating" the perpetrator really work?

When you turn to the person who offended you and point out their racism, they might think, *Well, gee-whiz! That wasn't my intention at all.* Or perhaps, *You're just being sensitive.* I chose the word *think* for a reason. It is rarely relevant what people say in these circumstances because it is unlikely to be genuine. Many professionals will apologize as a knee-jerk reaction if they happen to offend someone. Period, end of story, regardless of whether they truly understand why they need to apologize or agree that their behavior was offensive. Of course, not every microaggression perpetrator will even make a show of remorse. There are some individuals who *will* verbally go on the offensive, make excuses, or attempt to justify their actions.

As interesting as the verbal responses of some may be, their thought processes are more intriguing because oftentimes, not only do we want this person to stop behaving in an offensive manner, but we also may desire to develop and maintain a relationship with him or her. And sometimes, our entire career depends on it. All too often, regardless of their verbal response, the perpetrator walks away thinking, *Yikes. Mental note. Avoid that person. Too emotional.*

She is a hardworking mother of three, and she is not racist. She climbed a ladder of success she constructed with her own hard work, never able to "get ahead" with the simple deployment of the race card. She got into school because she won the dean over with her intellect, not the complexion of her skin. She herself was colorblind despite those around her whose vision was tainted by race, turning every matter into a racial one. No, she's definitely not racist.

He is a humble man dedicated to his religion, and he is not racist. Through his faith, he has remained unbiased all his life, treating the Black family in his ward all the same, making them feel more welcome if anything. A nod to Africa here, a reference to 2Pac there, occasionally throwing in phrases that *they* might be more familiar with. He pats the top of their youngest child's head each time he sees him—a fluffy fade, and he compliments the texture. His cousin's brother's husband is Black. No, he's definitely not racist.

He is a police officer, and he is not racist. He has three Black friends, and he loves watching the NBA. Last week, he apologized after he detained and handcuffed a Black woman and her four small children after allegedly mistaking her minivan for a stolen motorcycle from another state. No, he's not racist.

She is captain of her high school basketball team, and she is not racist. The Black girls on her team only inspire her. It's because of them that she decided to get cornrows and the reason she dressed up as Beyoncé for Halloween the year before. She envies the interesting names of some of her Black teammates and has adopted cool Black terms of endearment like "sista," "brotha," "homie," and more. She posts a photo of Malcolm X on Instagram during Black History Monday. No, she's definitely not racist.

The quagmire is that white people, like all human beings, gravitate toward individuals they understand and who understand them in return. The ultimate goal is to reach the point of mutual understanding, but the best time to tackle this is not in the moment we are offended. We need to be tactful. We must work to disarm the individual first, a topic we'll address later in this book.

We've all received countless questionable comments from white people over the years—too many to count. Here are a few examples that are illustrative of implicit bias:

They say: "You're so articulate."

A school administrator once said to me: "Wow! You are very articulate." It sounds like a genuine compliment at first, but there are, of course, many implications behind this statement. Racist implications. Notwithstanding the fact that I am indeed articulate, this comment seldom felt like a compliment. Each time I have received this backhanded compliment, it was clear that the person was surprised by my intellect and was not expecting me to be well-spoken. I didn't fit his or her racist stereotype, so the white person felt compelled to praise me for my astonishing display of communicative brilliance. Oftentimes, this comment would come at peculiar, disruptive moments, such as when I was in the middle of a sentence or after I had asked an important question. Can you imagine how ridiculous it would sound if I did the reverse to a white colleague in the midst of being given pertinent information? "Um, yes. I am articulate. Thanks. So, as I was saying..."

We think: As a Black person, it feels awkward at best to field haphazard comments about being generally articulate. Instead, if you absolutely must, try to compliment a specific aspect of what the person said or provide substantive positive feedback. Also, try not to sound so surprised.

They say: "You don't sound Black."

We think: *Please never say this. Like, please just don't.*

A job interviewer once actually said this to me. This statement is clearly offensive and blunter than the one above, but it essentially means the same thing. As crazy as it sounds, many white people actually intend such a comment as a compliment. They truly do not believe you sound "Black" and have an uncontrollable urge to share that with you, as if you won some kind of prize. Statements like this stem from a deeply rooted pattern of underestimating and undervaluing Black intelligence and language skills.

They say: "Racism is not my fault."

A friend's father told me that racism wasn't his problem or his fault, and he followed it with, "My ancestors never owned slaves." This is an absurdly tone-deaf, irrelevant statement. No rational person is looking to blame racism on any individual white person. Racism did not miraculously end on April 9, 1865 when General Robert E. Lee surrendered his Confederate troops to the Union's Ulysses S. Grant. Today, white people still benefit from the preceding 400 years of slavery, as well as from the systems and institutions that were founded on principles of slavery. Even by 1960, there were still twenty-one states with anti-miscegenation laws prohibiting interracial marriage—and Alabama did not repeal this law until the year 2000. Let that sink in.

We think: Listen with an open mind. Acknowledge your privilege, count your blessings, and commit yourself to doing what you can, big or small, to make this country safer and more equitable for Black citizens.

They say: "White privilege? What white privilege?"

A wealthy fund manager once told me, "White privilege does not exist. I scratched and clawed for my success." Achieving a life of personal and professional success is hard regardless of your skin color, so the phrase "white privilege" often triggers feelings of indignation. But in reality, white people dislike the term for two main reasons. First, the word "white" in and of itself makes white people uncomfortable because, ironically, white people are not accustomed to being generalized and defined by the color of their skin. This discomfort prompts them to make statements like, "I don't see color." Second, the word "privilege" is difficult to accept for the middle class, and it's especially hard to swallow for white folk in poor and rural areas. The word is perceived as an attack, an attempt to invalidate their life's greatest struggles and hard-won triumphs.

White defensiveness in the face of important discussions on racial issues derails the dialogue and distorts the critical message. Their propensity for defensiveness aside, white privilege is a powerful, invisible force that needs to be recognized. Having the freedom to walk around stores without being followed is a privilege. Having a majority of cosmetic products catered toward your hair type and skin tone by default is a privilege. Getting pulled over by the police for an actual reason is a privilege. Being treated fairly by your teachers is a privilege. Turning on the television and seeing people of your race widely represented is a privilege. Being able to protest without being attacked by federal agents, shot with rubber bullets, and arrested is a privilege.

We think: Having white privilege does not make you racist; it does not mean you have lived a struggle-free life, and it does not even necessarily mean you have relative affluence or access. No. Having white privilege means that you had a built-in advantage, regardless of what your subjective circumstances may be. Yes, white privilege is real, and its existence is fueled by historic, enduring racism and biases, factors that need to be recognized, acknowledged, and eliminated. Have you ever struggled because of the color of your skin?

They say: "All lives matter."

My neighbor has a sign outside her home that proclaims that statement, and I get to drive by it every day. Context is everything. This phrase, as technically correct as it may sound, is offensive. Saying "All lives matter" is effectively a protest to my protest. The "Black Lives Matter" movement does not mean "*only* Black lives matter"; it means "Black lives matter *too*." Those who oppose the racial justice movement and the phrase

"Black lives matter" are ignoring the racism exemplified in police interactions that end in the murders of Black Americans.

We think: Be sensitive to the pain of the people suffering in the moment. Consider this: if an office building were on fire, the fire department probably wouldn't spray thousands of gallons of water at every building on the block screaming, "All buildings matter." Or what about this? If you were at a funeral mourning the death of a close relative it would be equally inappropriate for someone to interrupt the eulogy and say, "All deaths matter. My dad died two years ago."

They say: "Focus on the pandemic."

A *friend* complained in a post on Facebook: "#BLM protests are stupid. What about the #COVID-19 pandemic? Did we all forget about that now?" Protesting during COVID-19 presents unique challenges and risks, which means we need to do so safely. But statements such as this invalidate the seriousness of the racial injustices that are being protested. The murder of George Floyd has once again brought the public crisis of racial injustice to the forefront. Racism results in concrete, quantifiable disparities in the health and wellness of Black Americans—a public crisis resulting in unequal access to medical care, livable wages, quality education, healthy food, and adequate housing.

We think: You're in a vehicle. If the person driving the vehicle tells you to put on your seatbelt, you absolutely should. But if the driver starts shooting the passengers, it's time to unbuckle. People of all races and ethnicities in our communities are calling for systemic change, and many have taken to the streets in safe, largely nonviolent protest. We have a First Amendment right to participate in such protests, and doing so presents a unique opportunity to stand in solidarity with those who have been affected by racism.

They say: "Stop the violence."

"It's horrible that an innocent Black man was killed, but destroying property and looting has to stop," a former law school classmate told me. This statement prioritizes the wrong part of what's happening and is leading many people to ignore the critical message. We need to remind them, as I reminded my former classmate, not to allow themselves to be distracted from focusing on the real issue.

Not "It's horrible that an innocent Black man was killed, but destroying property and looting has to stop," but "It is horrible that property is being destroyed, but killing innocent Black men has to stop."

Major social justice movements have a history of provoking some violence. Black Lives Matter has received harsh denigration from today's moderate and conservative pundits for its supporters' alleged use of "aggressive" tactics that "incite violence." Many have also been quick to point out that *our Black hero* Martin Luther King was a staunch supporter of nonviolent protest and speculate that he would disapprove of Black Lives Matter demonstrations. Garnering widespread attention for the movement is crucially important to creating awareness and promoting change, and it was certainly essential to King's approach during the Civil Rights Movement.

Have we all forgotten the violence that pervaded the Civil Rights era? Have we forgotten Emmett Till? Have we forgotten that Martin Luther King Jr. and Malcolm X were both assassinated? King's followers, Black and white, were American pioneers for justice. They marched through the hostile streets of 1960s America and were savagely beaten, attacked, arrested, and killed by police officers in the process. They marched day after day, aware of their violent fate, and some even invited it. Were they inciting violence? Many thought so, calling King's methods of protest too aggressive, claiming his message encouraged violence. In King's famous "Letter from Birmingham Jail," he clarified that his chief objective was "so to dramatize the issue that it can no longer be ignored."

King was not a supporter of violence, but he knew it was an expected, unavoidable consequence of justice denied. Human rights activists like King and John Lewis bravely endured violence, and it is because of their bravery that we enjoy the spoils of the Civil Rights Movement's success.

Lewis, who died in 2020, left a legacy of getting into "good trouble" to oppose racism. He also said, "Freedom is not a state; it is an act. It is not some enchanted garden perched high on a distant plateau where we can finally sit down and rest. Freedom is the continuous action we all must take, and each generation must do its part to create an even more fair, more just society."

The Black Lives Matter movement is about violence, and it is a response to violence. Never forget.

We think: Is there a form of protest that white supremacy will approve of? Please advise because we are quite literally dying to know.

They say: "I'm not racist. I have Black friends."

There is a difference between being racially prejudiced and racism in general. You may not have a conscious dislike for Black people, which is certainly a start.

But having a Black friend doesn't keep you from exhibiting biased behavior or insulate you from your failure to challenge the institution of racism.

We think: Believing you cannot be racist is tone deaf to the larger social framework. Just pause and take some time to listen—and try to avoid making sweeping generalizations or offer some shallow reasoning behind why you're not racist. Your individual intentions are important, but as long as you're complicit in racist ideologies, policies, and institutions, you still have some work to do.

They say: "Hey, can I touch your hair?"

I have been asked this easily one hundred times in my life. An aspect to this question is rooted in racism, and another aspect is that is simply a violation of personal boundaries. Given the history of Black people being treated as property or pets, this question makes us feel like animals on display.

We think: Would you ever ask blond, blue-eyed Larry from accounting that question? Probably not. But Black hair is cool; we get that. Being curious or having a sudden urge to touch our hair *almost* makes sense, and it is *almost* a compliment. But ultimately, it's not. It's a super weird, awkward, and inappropriate question. Please, never ask it.

They say: "I'm color blind."

During implicit bias training, a lawyer at a large law firm said this, and I've heard it, as I know you have, many other times. This statement is literally never true, but the person who says it wants it to be. The problem is that many white people who make this remark are trying to convey that they are opposed to acts of segregation and blatant discrimination. Nonetheless, they have dismissed, ignored, and made invisible Black issues under the guise of "color blindness."

> **We think**: We want you to see us. Saying you're "color blind" is counterproductive. Black people exist, and unless you have achromatopsia, you can probably tell. So, how about this? Just try to be less racist.

They say: "Hey, homeboy."

Brian, one of my younger siblings' white coworkers, is always calling them "Homie" or "Homeboy." These terms of endearment represent a relationship of familiarity and intimacy, but all too often, they are used to address Black people when there is no close or meaningful relationship between the parties whatsoever. While it's still inappropriate to act in such a way, the reason is usually harmless. It's a desperate and unfortunately unsuccessful attempt by white folk to relate to and connect with Black people.

We think: Regardless of race, nicknames are earned. One step at a time. If you don't know the person like that, just use their actual name.

I believe most white people are good and do not intend their racist microaggressions. Their frequent failure to understand the meaning and impact of their behavior presents an intriguing dilemma. On the one hand, as a Black man, I'm angered by the behavior of white folk, and I feel compelled to take swift, verbally punitive action. "Excuse me. That was racist because XYZ."

On the other hand, I am aware that confronting the person is highly unlikely to produce any favorable outcome.

Robin DiAngelo, author of a *New York Times* bestseller on race relations, is a professor, a diversity consultant, and a white woman. She argues that when whites in America are forced to face their racist biases, they experience feelings of resistance because of a concept she refers to as white fragility. DiAngelo, like many white "experts" on bias and racism, is well educated and knowledgeable. These experts usually have a PhD from an Ivy League university and an all-star resume exuding "experience" in the art of diversity and inclusion programming. They teach classes. They consult for Fortune 500 companies. They start nonprofits. They write books. They tell any white person who will listen how racist they are. They encourage white Americans to face themselves, self-analyze, and reflect on their hidden racist tendencies. They're "woke" white people. If you are an employee at a large company or a university student, you know what I'm talking about. You've almost certainly sat through an implicit bias training or presentation on diversity led by a white expert, and you may have been the only person of color in the room.

White folk have an easier time listening to white experts, so their prominence makes some sense. But I am not convinced. Despite presumably having sincere intentions, in the course of their efforts to dignify Black people, they diminish us. Similar to the unconscious bias that white experts see in all white folk, their own racism is unintentional. Still, despite good intentions, white experts like DiAngelo frequently fall short of the mark. Reading her book feels eerily similar to sitting through implicit bias training.

Like most training programs led by white experts, the perspectives contained in her book are mostly correct. DiAngelo has dedicated her career to curing white people of their racism and, in her book, shares her experiences conducting bias training. These experiences primarily involve making white people cry, shout, or head straight for the exit—and sometimes all of the above—as she helps them face their racism.

First of all, the dynamic of white experts preaching on the subject of bias to a congregation consisting of mainly white people is interesting and very awkward. In a room of twenty or thirty, I'm usually one of only a handful of Black people. I'm sure that's fairly typical, but it presents a backward and perverse situation.

Should men be the intellectual ambassadors on how sexism and gender bias impacts women? Would it be awkward to be one of two women in a training session with thirty white men? Would it be even worse if the training were being led by a white man?

"Let me explain how women feel. Let me tell you about the female experience. Women feel like X when men do Y."

Perhaps this is an accurate comparison to how similar dynamics have made me feel. But after all, I cannot be certain. Because I am a man, I will never truly understand how it feels to be a woman. No matter how much research I perform. No matter how many studies I read. No matter how many degrees I obtain.

White experts carry themselves like missionaries, preaching the good word of white wokeness and seeing themselves as messengers of a magnificent wisdom that the unenlightened fail to perceive. Yet it is often clear that they themselves have failed to look inward and discover that they still have a great deal to learn.

Worse, though, is that they often dismiss and discount our opinions and ideas. I recently witnessed a white expert actively talk over a Black man who was trying to share his perspective during a bias training. She asked a leading question that had a presumptuous answer. "Black people feel like this, right?" The white expert was guiding the conversation and clearly had an ideal response in her mind. "No, actually, I don't because..." The man disagreed with the premise of the question and attempted to explain how she had faltered. She would not have it. His response did not track her own ideologies about how Black people feel. It did not perfectly match up with her well-organized PowerPoint presentation. She ignored him and moved on. She was the expert after all.

The man looked over at me with a humorous expression that said, *Haha! Is she fucking kidding me?* I looked back at him with a shrug and a sarcastic smile, shaking my head.

DiAngelo's book is a great example of this because it is chock-full of erroneous theories and opinions sadly detached from reality. She implies in her book that white women crying in response to being called racist reminds Black people of the history of white women crying as they lied about being raped by Black men. Really? Is this true? How does she actually know? Perhaps when white women cry while dealing with their racism *she* is in fact reminded of Black men raping women. Which would be...not great.

DiAngelo ordains herself as the authority on what is required to measure up to the bar of existing as a non-fragile white person—that is, a white person who is inoffensive to Black people. A white person who is not racist. She claims using the term "bad" in reference to a certain neighborhood is actually code for "Black" neighborhood, but if you say that a neighborhood is "Black," you're racist because what you're really insinuating is that the neighborhood is "bad." Thus, by DiAngelo's logic, it would appear that referring to Black neighborhoods *or* bad neighborhoods whatsoever is forbidden and highly offensive to Black people. Again, is this true? Are there not predominantly Black neighborhoods? And completely separately, are there not neighborhoods rife with crime that could be reasonably labeled bad?

White experts are well-intentioned but often misguided, presenting their own narrative on how it feels to be Black and making bold assumptions—too many assumptions—about how Black people should be treated. DiAngelo and other white experts frequently propagate a deeply condescending portrayal of the Black community, striking a tone that is profoundly patronizing to Black people.

Racism has affected me deeply, as it has the entire Black community. But this is our story to tell, and it is our decision whether, how, and when to tell it. There is no prosperity in weakness. Black people neither need nor want anyone to muse over white privilege because this approach only exacerbates the fallacy of white superiority. The Black community is strong, and we are rising. Power is made by power being taken. We neither need nor want white pity. We neither need nor want white guilt. We neither need nor want pandering white experts regardless of how well-meaning they may be.

Can we have this? Can Black people have this one thing? Can Black people be afforded the domain of expertise on Blackness?

White experts like DiAngelo often have what is commonly referred to as a white "savior" or "messiah" complex. This phenomenon is highly prevalent in the diversity and inclusion movement, chiefly promulgated by large, predominantly white corporations. These "white savior"-led programs result in approaches that are more rooted in promoting charity than justice. They hinder the mission's progress and prevent the process from being dialogical and participatory. White experts swoop in to rescue Black people from peril with their self-righteous, sanctimonious solutions while failing to include and listen to the voices of Black leaders and organizations.

POVERTY PORN

Diversity and inclusion initiatives embolden white paternalism, thus motivating white folk to think of anti-racism as philanthropy instead of seeking to empower and build local capacity. This circumstance turns white people into heroes rather than allowing Black people to become the heroes of their own lives. It robs the Black community of meaningful choice and promotes a Black identity grounded in shame, vulnerability, and helplessness. It is the same misperception of Blackness that induces white folks to fly to Africa and take selfies with Black children and post them on social media. This twisted practice can only be defined as poverty porn, perpetuating ubiquitous images and ideas that objectify Blackness, labeling us as powerless victims who can't help ourselves.

There is a deeper disease that afflicts my Black brothers and sisters, but in order to see it, we must work to move beyond making fledgling attempts to cure the symptoms of racism with white guardian angels. The Black community welcomes white allies and anti-racists to join our fight against racism. Reflecting on the history of white colonialism and current systems that promote and enable white privilege is important. But whites who graduate from the process of self-reflection and guilt are not bequeathed with any expert qualifications on the sensitivity of Black feelings.

TRAUMA PORN

We continue to decry police violence in American cities. The murders of Jacob Blake, George Floyd, Breonna Taylor, Atatiana Jefferson, and many others have sparked national outrage. Still, this videotaped, photographed, or written media exploits traumatic moments of Black pain to generate buzz and media attention. This phenomenon can only be described as trauma porn, a timeless and perverse fascination with Black suffering.

White people often argue, "But those viral videos spread awareness!" Yes, it is indisputable that viral images and videos of Black murders at the hands of police have played a substantial role in advancing dialogue surrounding racial injustice. However, sharing disturbing videos is neither virtuous nor white allyship, and it traumatizes us. Our oppression need not be validated by graphic videos on the internet. White allyship requires more than spreading awareness. True white allyship requires the execution of a strategy capable of dismantling the intolerant, oppressive systems that plague Black communities.

Trauma porn desensitizes the world to Black suffering. Videos of Black people being brutalized or killed by police have become widely popularized. This shameless, flagrant consumption of Black misery is eerily reminiscent of lynching barbecues of the not-so-distant early 1900s. It seems like every week, we see a new video depicting a modern-day lynching. The frequency and nature of how this media is consumed is tantamount to a TV series, with each Black person murdered a new episode. White folk all tune in, consume Black pain, and comment on the horror with shock and awe.

Other white folks argue, "But sharing these videos forces the hand of justice by creating public anger."

These murders do not occur in isolation. They're an intended result of a system that was designed to oppress and destroy the Black population. The indictment and sentencing of police officers responsible for these murders only solves part of the problem. We can't arrest the murder weapon; there can be no meaningful change until the current system of policing is dismantled and rebuilt. It's like eliminating a pawn in a game of chess; there can be no victory until we take down the king.

Consuming media that depicts Black deaths on social media will not save Black lives. We need to make it clear that before sharing this content, people should first consider the following: Why am I sharing this? Besides sharing this content, what else am I doing, or willing to do, to dismantle the system of white supremacy? Do I vote in every election? Have I contacted my local representatives? Have I donated to organizations committed to racial justice? What am I doing to combat racism at my workplace or school? Am I supporting Black businesses and professionals? What books or educational media have I read to educate myself on anti-racism? Is there something other than this viral video of a Black person being murdered that could be more helpful to share? These are the questions people need to ask themselves.

BLACK RESILIENCE

Our mistreatment does not define us. The pain we've suffered, the trials we've endured...they do not define us. We, the Black women and men of this country, are going to define our own identity. We—you—are Black and resilient. You will be knocked down. When you are, bounce back up. Anticipate and adapt. Keep going, no matter what. We can't change the past, but we can plan for a better future. We must count, weigh, and analyze all threats to our personal and professional goals with meticulous care.

While we must never ignore racism, we must not allow white privilege to dominate the narrative on what it means to be Black. Our mistreatment does not define us. The pain we've suffered, the trials we've endured... they do not define us. We, the Black women and men of this country, are going to define our own identity.

CHAPTER 3

BUILDING BLACK IDENTITY: TEARING DOWN THE MYTHS

WHEN SHE WAS THREE, A little Black girl dreamed of being an astronaut. She'd explore the vastness and wonder of the universe and discover all the secrets that lay within. She'd gaze through telescopes and analyze "space dust" collected from the sandbox. She investigated relentlessly until she found the answer to every question she had. But then her parents laughed and rolled their eyes and doubt crept in. When she was eight, the little Black girl became entranced with math. She could calculate faster than anyone else in her class. She was going to be a mathematician. She'd solve problem after problem, maybe even develop mathematical theories or crack codes that no one else could. But then her teacher said that math would only become more difficult the older she got and that she should set a more realistic goal.

When she was thirteen, the Black girl was determined to be a teacher. She'd educate the supposedly unteachable students, and they would carry the lessons she imparted years after their last class. But then her friends questioned if she was smart enough to teach, and doubt crept in.

When she was eighteen, the young Black woman wanted to graduate from high school. She'd be the first of her family to wear that cap and gown, to waltz across that stage and grip the diploma with sweet satisfaction. But then she got pregnant, and her boyfriend reassured her that he'd provide for them, so why even bother with school?

When she was three, the little Black girl dreamed of being an astronaut.

She wanted to be seen. All human beings have this innate need. We want our peers, our superiors, our teachers, and our friends to not just look at us but to see us for who we truly are and to believe that we can accomplish whatever we set our minds to. We want others to accurately perceive us, and we want to be given the benefit of the doubt. We want the world to see our children as future leaders: future scholars, lawyers, doctors, and engineers. We want our children to be seen as capable of achieving anything they set out to do. Everyone wants this—regardless of race, age, gender, sexual orientation, religion, or class.

Naturally, we all want to be seen. But too many people of color feel forced to wear a mask, a figurative mask of assimilation, aimed at minimizing their differences to appear "inoffensive" and relatable. Being treated differently as a child merely because of the color of your skin causes deeply embedded trauma that is difficult to overcome. Each microaggression and instance of mistreatment can lodge itself within your psyche. These seeds of doubt have potential to germinate. And as you grow older, the doubts grow and grow, eventually setting arbitrary psychological limits on your potential, stifling your self-confidence and choking out all promise.

The roots of racism and bias run deep; they have a range of different categories and subtypes. Some instances are explicit, like the use of racial slurs, hate speech, or laws that deliberately victimize people because of their skin color. Other types are more subversive yet hidden in plain sight. These cases of prejudice are obscured and often subconscious. Implicit or subconscious bias appreciably falls into the latter category. The person doling out this unethical treatment may be oblivious to their own deep-rooted racism. Whether it's latent or obvious, one thing is for certain: regardless of its form or variety, racism hurts. It's hurt me, and I'm sure it's hurt you.

But your identity should not be governed by racist ideologies. Your identity is not something that should be controlled or dictated by others. Ideally, the truth of your identity exists outside of others' biased perceptions.

Bias and identity go hand in hand. The amalgamation of an individual's personal characteristics, values, memories, experiences, and relationships are the building blocks of who each of us are. These ingredients encompass our sense of self, providing a baseline for how we will perceive ourselves and, in turn, how others will perceive us. As we develop, new facets of our identity emerge and are incorporated into our sense of self over time.

Bias has inherently harmful effects on our lives; it negatively influences the way we think of ourselves, which further impedes the way others perceive us, effecting a vicious cycle of self-doubt. Our thought process dictates reality. Positive thinking is powerful and results in positive outcomes, so naturally, negative thinking is equally as powerful and results in negative outcomes. So how does one refuse to accept an identity inescapably bound to the dreadful conditions of racism? We must learn to define and proudly display our own identity as opposed to allowing it to be defined by others. Hold on tight and never let go. Never give up the image of yourself that others attempt to undermine.

THE IDENTITY EQUATION

The journey to exploring our identity often begins with an important and existential question: "Who am I?" A simple query with an exceedingly complicated answer.

Identity includes immutable characteristics like height, race, and temporary circumstances, such as socioeconomic class. Identity also encompasses political opinions, moral attitudes, and religious beliefs. These core components of our identity guide the decisions we make on a daily basis. People who feel that they are not able to fully or accurately express a key aspect of their identity are frequently concerned with what others think of them.

Almost every day I can remember, I have been told that I look like a basketball player. Strangers, even now, stop me in the street to ask me how tall I am and where I played. This is fine, of course, and I'm never the least bit offended. I'm absurdly tall, and for most of my life, I did play basketball. I was seen as Braeden Anderson, the basketball player. But my mother saw me as Braeden Anderson, her child—her tall son who was capable of being anything. Her tall son who was capable of being an entrepreneur, a doctor, a lawyer, an accountant, a

CEO, a tech executive, or a hedge fund manager. Black girls, boys, men, women, non-binary folks, and those of all shapes and sizes can excel at anything.

I don't care where you grew up. I don't care what shade of Black you are. I don't care what your sexual orientation is. I don't care if you're the first person in your family to go to college. I don't care what your grades are. I don't even care if you have a criminal record.

There is a plan for you. There is a way forward. You can study and learn what steps you need to take, execute them, achieve any goal you set your mind to, and overcome any obstacle or challenging circumstance. You are powerful and resilient.

If you're in college and aspire to be an accountant, not only can you land a job at a Big Four accounting firm, but you can make partner.

If you're in high school and have a dream of becoming a doctor, you can get into the medical school of your choice and match with a top-ranked residency program in the specialization of your choosing.

If you're a basketball player who wants to be a lawyer one day, you can get law school paid for while you win a Big East championship and then land a job at a major Big Law firm.

Whatever it is you want to accomplish, you can do it.

When we perceive that the beliefs others have about our identity are negative, our thoughts are misdirected. We are led to inaccurate understandings of who we are and what we are capable of. The process of self-reflection and analysis is critical to the identity equation. The most powerful catalyst for personal growth hinges on the discrepancy regarding three important variables:

Who you are.

Who you want to be.

Who you could be.

This is the identity equation. Your ideas about yourself matter. The beliefs you hold about your personal potential either drive you forward or hold you back.

People generally have an exceedingly narrow-minded vision of what they believe can be accomplished based on their current circumstances or temporary environmental conditions; this is a narrow-minded version of their potential limited by crippling self-doubt and false philosophies about the implausibility of our desires.

These factors have the effect of setting artificial limits on your potential based on socioeconomic status, race, how you were raised, what your parents told you, and what your friends say.

Often when we share our ambitions with the world, we are met with doubt, criticism, or outright rejection. A negative comment from a friend, boss, colleague, coach, or loved one can have extraordinary power—the power to prevent us from even trying to achieve our goals.

You must seek to shatter the false, negative perceptions you harbor about yourself and destroy the implicit biases that others project onto you.

My painful experiences with various forms of racism have fortunately provided me with a unique perspective on how to successfully navigate race-related obstacles. They have also instilled in me an unshakeable desire to share my insight with others.

As an adjunct professor, I open the first class of each semester with an explanation of why I became a lawyer, a description of what it is like, and a general encouragement to the class to consider applying to law school. Many of my Black students reply with statements like, "I would love to do that, but I can't."

I always respond with some variation of, "Really? Why? Walk me through your reasoning."

After this investigative questioning, not a single student who immediately rejected the idea is able to reasonably substantiate their claim. The goal of this line of questioning is to teach them to be just as critical of their negative ideas about themselves as others tend to be of positive ideas—criticism that may be explicit or implicit. When we make statements that are highly positive about ourselves, society is quick to ask tough questions and to criticize. This is unfortunate but natural and predictable. Be ready for it.

Our parents are quick to share their concerns, and our friends don't hesitate to voice their doubts. After being repeatedly faced with these reactions, we are more inclined to embrace familiar, negative ideas. In many cases, these comments are a reflection of the other person's insecurities. They are often a projection of the reasons why that person believes they themselves are unworthy. While these negative comments are not usually intended to bring us down, they often do.

Effective critical thinking demands that we treat both positive and negative ideas honestly and objectively and that we eliminate our biases. Before we can urge the world to eliminate negative biases about our identity and what we are capable of, we first need to eliminate our own. My current professional and academic achievements were frankly unfathomable ten years ago. My life outcome does not really make sense, at least not by any common or practical metric.

Don't get it twisted; we need to be objective. We all have a duty to think objectively, reasonably, and pragmatically. We need to be logical. We need to truly champion these characteristics, and while we think we do, we often don't. When I was in college, I confided in a friend and teammate about my intention to go to law school one day and become a lawyer. He was mesmerized by the idea and asked me dozens of questions about how I planned on doing it.

"That sounds awesome. I could never do that, though," he said.

"Why not?" I asked. "You have good grades."

"You're light-skinned, bro," he said with a shrug. "I'm too Black to make it at any of those white law firms."

There are not many light-skinned brothers at these firms either, I thought. I was momentarily discouraged, but then I remembered something despite all my present self-doubt. Every point has a counterargument—a philosophy I was instilled with in my childhood. I grew up amidst a family who could never resist a good debate. Every point brought up in conversation had the potential to be cross-examined. A multitude of family dinners began and ended with a passionate debate on current events. One time a friend came over and after a rousing discussion on whether a community's water source should be fluoridated or not, he looked uncomfortable. When we were alone he said, "That was intense! You guys sure fight a lot." I found this reaction funny in that I hadn't considered our hearty family debates to be out of the ordinary. These experiences led to critical analysis of my own opinions and allowed me to combat negative self-talk with my own counterargument. I thought again about my friend's excuse. My rebuttal would be executed in the form of my future success. I repeated the mantra that I was built for this. I was ready to fight for what I wanted. Others' preconceived notions of what was achievable in life would not deter me.

I learned to digest and accept the opinions of others carefully and very selectively. Whether these opinions were related to racism or not, I was quick to challenge ideas that did not resonate with me and ask vigilant questions. As I have embarked on my own journeys, both in law and as an athlete, I have been told many stories of my failure. My goals have been criticized, laughed at, and dismissed as silly, "childish" dreams. But scary tales are not enough to deter me. I was on a mission, and I was not going to stop until my objective was reached. I made a promise to myself that I would never stop fighting, that I would never quit.

I was built for this, and so were you. You too must make the same promise to yourself. You too must set a course and relentlessly fight until you reach your destination.

When we do not see ourselves properly represented, it casts doubt on our own potential. When we do not see enough people "like us" who have done something, it's hard to imagine ourselves doing it. When only 2 percent of executives at a given company are Black, it makes us feel like we only have about a 2 percent chance of getting there. But is that true? What do statistics really mean?

When I concocted the idea of playing basketball while in law school, the statistics did not suggest that my dream was possible. The data clearly showed that there was not a single men's NCAA basketball player in law school. Not one. Many in whom I confided and asked for advice drew the obvious conclusion: "Well, it cannot be done." Their response took the form of a quick, simple dismissal. "Nope. Move on. Next idea." But I was not willing to be dissuaded so easily. I was not ready to admit the "obvious" conclusion. Not yet. Giving up because a goal does not appear to be possible stems from the evolution of a pervasive fallacy in the way many people approach problems.

Exactly zero percent of current NCAA division 1 college basketball players were in law school at the time. But what does that mean exactly? While it was true that there was nobody currently doing it, I needed to add some other variables to this equation. I needed to add more data. For any statistic to be relevant to a particular hypothesis, there must be some qualifying correlation between it and the data source. Here is the primary fact: you do not have even the remote possibility of playing basketball while in law school, the reason being the rules stated that you are only allowed four years of eligibility to play in the NCAA. After getting an undergraduate degree, a requirement for law school, you simply won't have any years left; this is true, of course, unless you are graduating at least one year early and have at least one year of eligibility remaining. I was on track to graduate with two years of eligibility remaining, so what percentage of men's NCAA division 1 basketball players graduated two years early? Maybe no one. Maybe one or two individuals. We could even widen our sample set and identify how many NCAA student athletes graduated or were on track to graduate one year early. This category of individuals was relatively small, but there were certainly at least a few dozen. How many in that pool had a predetermined desire to play basketball while in law school? And even further, how many had tried and been rejected? How many people are there in your "goal" category who have failed? If statistically no one, or very few, have failed, how can any statistic of zero percent accurately apply to you? The farther I walked down that path of critical thinking and reflection, the more I realized that I was utterly alone. That epiphany left me feeling vulnerable and anxious. But I was also deeply excited because I knew my goal could still be theoretically achievable. I knew there was no adequate sample set to which I could anchor any meaningful statistic. I knew there was a chance it could be done, and I believed passionately that if anyone could do it, I could.

We have to be willing to embark on the hero's journey. As you may know, Joseph Campbell, the great mythologist, wrote *The Hero with a Thousand Faces*, *The Power of Myth*, and *The Inner Reaches of Outer Space*, in which he compared the myths and legends of various cultures. He created a metaphor for the transformation from embarking on the journey, encountering challenges, reaching the point of near destruction, then going for broke, and returning home changed, and he called this transforming experience the Hero's Journey. It's serious, real stuff that moves through the ages, from stories told around a campfire to the *Star Wars* series, which George Lucas, who greatly admired Campbell's work, created based on that journey.

We have to be able to pursue a similar course: to harbor an attitude that reflects a willingness to fearlessly confront uncomfortable situations, trials, and tribulations, to develop a complete knowledge of ourselves that embodies total confidence in our own limitless potential.

We need to be critical of perspectives from parents, peers, or anyone else regarding what is deemed "realistic" for us.

Priscilla Mayowa, a dual-enrollment student at North Hennepin Community College and Bemidji State University in Minnesota, moved to the United States from Nigeria. In both high school and college, Mayowa felt that teachers assumed she didn't know things and that they judged her more harshly for mistakes than they did her white peers. As a result, she developed imposter syndrome and feared being exposed as a fraud. Although her goal was initially to go to law school, Mayowa was pushed by college advisors to apply to a nursing program, one that enrolls many Black women. Unwilling to settle for less than she wanted, she changed course. Now, with the help of a Black mentor, she is moving ahead on her own path, not the one others arbitrarily decided she should follow.[1]

Mentoring can indeed make a significant difference. A study took place involving 679 African American ninth-graders from urban environments and focused on how their choice of role models related to substance use, delinquency, academic engagement, and psychological well-being. Researchers found that male adolescents without male role models and females identifying brothers as role models reported the most problematic

---

1   Madeline St. Amour. "What Happens Before College Matters," *Inside Higher Ed*, October 20, 2020, https://www.insidehighered.com/ news/2020/10/20/black-students-need-changes-policies-and-structures-beyond-higher-education.

behavior. Adolescents with paternal male role models had the most positive school outcomes. The presence of female role models was associated with psychological well-being, and adolescents with maternal role models reported the least distress. Adolescents without female role models had the lowest grades and most negative school attitudes. These findings remained when parental support, family conflict, and father presence in the household were controlled, which suggests role model effects are separate from parenting effects.[2] This shows us that having someone to be a role model is vital. The power a mentor can have in the life of another individual can be great.

I was blessed to have role models who made a big difference in my life. Although my journey has been rife with adversity and overwhelming challenges, there were people in my family I could look up to. I had multiple relatives with graduate degrees, which was a distinct privilege, and I would be remiss not to recognize it as such. Even though we had different-colored skin, and thus surely had different experiences in the Canadian school system, my Opa and my uncle were tremendous resources for me. They had achieved a high level of aca-

2   Bryant, Alison L. and Marc A. Zimmerman. "Role Models and Psychosocial Outcomes Among African American Adolescents," *Journal of Adolescent Research* 18, no. 1 (2003): 36-67, doi: 10.1177/0743558402238276.

demic success, so I trusted their opinions. Even when I was performing very poorly in school, they always had confidence in my potential and relentlessly encouraged me to do better.

In tenth grade, just before I immigrated to the United States, I went to visit my uncle in Florida. I was equal parts thrilled to see him and to escape the freezing tundra that is Alberta, Canada in the winter. Over the course of my week-long visit, my uncle took me to watch Miami Heat NBA basketball games, to go shopping in South Beach, to eat dinners on the beach, and to let me drive fancy cars. That week was the first taste I ever had of luxury and wealth, and it had an impact on me. My uncle did not come from money, and his path was not paved with gold. He earned excellent grades and put himself through medical school with student loans and hard work, with very little support or guidance. Because he was white, he did have innate privilege. Even though he did not look like me and could not always relate to my struggles, he became my hero and role model all the same.

On the last day of my trip, we had a serious discussion about my life goals—and my poor grades. He ran through the usual speech at first.

"Do your very best, Braeden. I know that your current grades are not the best you can do."

This time was somehow different, though. What I'd had the privilege to experience that week had changed me. So, I asked the question that would change my life forever.

"Do you think I could become a doctor?" This was a critical question; I knew how hard he had worked to get where he was, and I trusted him to give me an honest answer. I genuinely expected him to say something like, "Well, maybe. But it would be really hard. Perhaps you could be a physician's assistant or something." That would be completely reasonable and rooted in reality. I asked him this question to prove to him that school was not worth my extra effort because I had a lower ceiling than he did—I could never become a doctor. I personally did not believe it was an attainable goal. I was already halfway through high school, falling behind with failing grades, and I had taken none of the pre-med prerequisites. But my uncle responded without hesitation or a hint of doubt.

"Yes, of course you could become a doctor!"

He said it with passion. He said it with confidence. He said it like he really fucking meant it. I sat there staring at him for a moment, analyzing his body language, trying to make sure he was being serious. *Hmm, could it be? Could he be right?* I still had my doubts, but I could tell that he believed what he was selling.

"Fine, then," I said. "I will do my best. I promise to do my very best in school from now on."

And from that moment forward, I did. I did my very best. While this vow did not immediately translate into getting straight As, or even Bs, gradually, the Ds turned into Cs, the Cs turned into Bs, and the Bs turned into As. More importantly, as my grades improved, I began to think of myself as smart. I began to think of myself as a good student. Other students began to recognize it, and my teachers did, too. This changed the status quo. It altered my identity and the way I saw myself. Of course, I would later choose to become a lawyer instead. But this commitment to doing my best in hopes of eventually becoming a doctor was exactly the push I needed. I knew that if I could defeat the negative opinions I had about myself and what I could reasonably accomplish, nothing could stop me. All that mattered was that I believed in myself and did my very best.

"You cannot be what you cannot see." This saying deeply resonated with me then, as a teenager questioning his academic worth, and it still does today. I am now compelled to see this concept manifest in the lives of those around me. If you cannot see and experience up close what could become of your hard work with your own senses, it is very difficult to truly believe that your success could be possible. This phrase is not intended to discount the accomplishments of pioneers and visionaries, and it does not mean that you literally cannot become something if you have not witnessed it. Still, it is indisputable that positive examples from leaders inspire us and allow us to dream of our own limitless potential. When your race is not represented in a profession or an entire industry, you have difficulty picturing yourself making it there. We are often left woefully unaware of the possibilities and unable to fathom becoming what we have not seen people who look like us or are similarly situated as us become.

You can become what you have not seen. You can be the role model that you desperately needed. You can change the course of history and inspire future generations with your example.

For years, I did not see my uncle as someone who was like me. I did not see his example as something that could ever be imitated by someone who was like me. Someone who looked like me. Someone who had my grades. Someone who grew up where I did. Someone who was treated by teachers the way I was treated. Unfortunately, Black people are often left with the inability to even think they can "reach for the stars" in the way of a career path.

Many of these professional environments are dominated by white people, people who we perceive as "not like us." We do not doubt that we could become professional athletes. We have seen dozens of professional athletes come from our own neighborhoods. We do not doubt that we could become recording artists or rappers. We have seen dozens of recording artists and rappers come from our own neighborhoods. We doubt what we have not yet seen.

At the beginning of this chapter, I talked about a little girl who wanted to be an astronaut. I was thinking about Katherine Johnson, Dorothy Vaughan, and Mary Jackson, who are portrayed in Margot Lee Shetterly's *Hidden Figures,* a book—later adapted into a film—about Black women working as mathematicians at the National Aeronautics and Space Administration during the Space Race. Those women were pioneers. Taking that journey starts not with some bootstrap philosophy that makes us feel we're somehow lacking because we can't succeed on our own but by knowing ourselves and what we're capable of. It starts by shutting out the noise, even the well-meaning noise of those who love us, and figuring out who we are, what we want to be, and what it's going to take to get us there.

It is up to us to create examples for those who follow us—to be someone who Black folks can look to as they embark on their own Hero's Journey.

CHAPTER 4

DEPLOYING TACTFUL EMPATHY: OUR COVERT OPERATION

TACT IS THE POWER TO communicate and behave in a manner that contemplates the feelings and reactions of others. Through pairing this technique with empathy, we can personify the truth of our identity and purpose while we conquer distracting, negative opinions of others in the process. Employing tactful empathy is a skill, and to master it, you need five essential elements: compassion, emotional intelligence, self-awareness, thoughtfulness, and diplomacy. Grasping these five skills will enable you to proficiently maneuver conversations dealing with sensitive topics. It will allow you to provide difficult feedback. Most important, it will help you adroitly choreograph a plan to overcome almost any form of racism or bias. Even in the face of intense adversity, employing a strategy rooted in tactful empathy will help you establish the identity you intend. Tactful empathy is a powerful tool that will allow you to create and preserve consequential relationships despite any initial hostility. In the wise words of Sir Isaac Newton, "Tact is the art of making a point without making an enemy."

Feelings of frustration and resentment in response to microaggressions are a fundamental part of the brain's threat response. Our brains' threat-detection mechanism involves sending signals to the amygdala, which processes our emotional responses. The amygdala, in turn, sends signals to the hypothalamus, which transmits signals to the adrenal glands to release powerful hormones like epinephrine (adrenaline) and cortisol. This triggers physical responses in the body in preparation to either quickly retreat or attack. As such, our brains are highly sensitive to perceived threats, leading to the frequent overestimation of dangers. This threat-detection mechanism is commonly referred to as the "fight or flight" response, which can be invoked by varying levels of perceived harms.

Humans are social animals, instilled with an instinctive desire to be approved of by others, to get along with others, and to be around others. When Black people feel victimized and abused in a social situation, the feeling typically triggers a threat response in their brains. White people experience a similar response when they feel criticized or judged. Although being chased by a bear may trigger a greater hormonal release than being verbally abused, criticized, or judged, these "less threatening" stimuli still trigger a considerable physical response in the body. Furthermore, the threat response restricts blood flow to important areas of the brain, limiting our ability to think, to be observant of others, and to be empathetic. Each of these functions is highly critical to accomplishing the goal of building and maintaining positive relationships, whether that be with our supervisors, our colleagues, our teachers, or any other person. Thus, in our efforts to defend ourselves against and subsequently address someone's bias, poor behavior, or microaggression, we must avoid triggering a threat response in that person.

In the second semester of my freshman year of college, I enrolled in an introductory level political science class: "PLSI 150 - Public Policy Making," taught by Dr. Mark Somma. As a self-described "future lawyer" and then political science major, I could hardly wait to sink my teeth into a substantive class that I was actually interested in, a class I believed would help me along on my journey to become the person I knew I could be. Dr. Mark Somma was a brilliant, highly regarded professor, one I had carefully chosen after evaluating his prior students' reviews on RateMyProfessor.com.

On the first day of class, we had basketball practice at the Save Mart Center from 11:00 a.m. until 3:00 p.m., right before my political science class. Other mandatory team activities that morning included weightlifting at 6:00 a.m., a shooting workout at 8:00 a.m., and a pre-practice film session at 10:00 a.m. Practice was eight-tenths of a mile from McKee Fisk, where class was located. I estimated that it was a fifteen-minute walk, or an eight-minute run. That day, as was the case most days, I had to run in order to make it to class.

Practice went late because we kept missing free throws during a conditioning drill at the end of practice, which led to extra suicide sprints. If you're fortunate enough to be unaware of what this drill entails, let me explain: a "suicide" involves repeatedly sprinting from the baseline to each of a series of four lines that run across the width of the basketball court. You run from the baseline to the free throw line and back, baseline to half court and back, baseline to opposite free throw line and back, baseline to opposite baseline and back. This equals one suicide. For NCAA-level athletes, suicides are usually timed—and if you do not complete each suicide in the requisite amount of time, it does not count.

To make the drill more difficult, many coaches choose to group suicides together into sets, usually of four or eight. In order to work on pressure free throws while battling fatigue, our coaches required that everybody make two consecutive free throws at the end of each set. If you or a teammate missed a free throw, the set did not count. That day, like many days prior, we missed a lot of free throws. And we ran a lot of suicides. Too many to count. Suffice it to say, forty or fifty suicides at the end of a four-hour practice are grueling—but standard.

After my teammates and I finished our final suicide, I grabbed my backpack and started sprinting in the direction of McKee Fisk. Practice ended fifteen minutes late, and class started at 3:20 p.m. My legs were trembling, I had a headache (likely dehydration-related), and I was drenched in sweat. But I had only five minutes to get there, so I didn't have time to shower or change clothes. I arrived at my first class with Dr. Mark Somma in the same manner I often arrived at class: disheveled, sporting smelly basketball shorts and a sweaty tank top, completely exhausted...and late.

When I walked in, the professor was already lecturing. But, as I scurried to find a seat, he paused and stared at me, just to make sure that we were all aware of his disapproval. He appreciated neither my appearance nor my tardiness. He continued his introductory remarks, described the structure of the class, and concluded by giving a standard "this class is not for everyone" sermon. In the course of this fervent rant, he repeated the above statement at least a half-dozen times, and he made an uncomfortable amount of passive-aggressive eye contact with me. Suffice it to say, Dr. Somma did not *see* me. He did not understand who I was or who I would be. Instead, he saw my sweaty clothes and late arrival, and he made up his mind that "this class is not for everyone—and certainly isn't for you."

Two weeks later, I turned in my first paper. I was conscious that Dr. Somma likely had some misapprehensions about my identity, and as such, I was eager to deliver an excellent work product. I was eager to show him who I was. I was eager to prove that I belonged in his class. The paper I wrote, to the best of my recollection, concerned how political parties influence public policy. To this day, I regret not saving the paper because now, I would frame it. And not because I received a good grade; quite the opposite, actually. Dr. Somma gave my paper an "F."

I stared at the ugly, red letter in utter disbelief for what felt like an eternity, completely blindsided. I had made the honor roll the prior semester, and I was feeling myself a bit. In hindsight, over the nearly ten years since that moment, my paper was not perfect, but it was certainly worthy of a "B."

When the class period ended, I walked to the front of the room, dropped the paper on Dr. Somma's desk, and simply asked, "How?"

His next words were shocking to me at the time. But honestly, they should not have been. He looked at me smugly and said, "Nice try. You did not write this."

As this sentence left his lips, I froze, dumbfounded. I searched for the words, a quick retort, but nothing came. Eventually, I simply said, "What? Yes, I did."

"Nah." He shook his head. "And I'm not sure this class is right for you."

At this point, I was seeing red. *Fuck this guy and fuck this class*, I thought.

So, I shot back, "Yeah, I think you're right," and proceeded to storm out of the classroom, slamming the door behind me.

I do not blame Dr. Somma for doubting me. Perhaps he had never before encountered a six-foot-eight, Black, Division I basketball player who was more than capable of writing an "A" paper. But I do blame him for the inept way he chose to confront me about his doubts. If he had engaged me with tactful empathy, he would have been more effective, despite his obvious biases. For example, he could have quizzed me about the ideas and opinions I expressed in the paper and engaged me in an academic discussion. If he were correct that someone else had written the paper for me, I would likely be unable to verbalize and discuss the substantive issues described therein. And if he were wrong, his quiz would be easily disguised as mere interest in my writing and my development as a student.

I immediately emailed the paper to my gastrointestinal surgeon uncle in Miami and to my Opa, a double PhD in psychology and education. I trusted their opinions and needed to be sure that I was not crazy for thinking an "F" was far outside the range of what I deserved. I did not tell them what grade I had received, but I sent them both a description of the assignment and asked them to read my work product carefully for both substance and grammar.

"Wow, this is terrific. Your writing keeps getting better and better," my uncle said.

"Braeden. Thanks for sending. Very well written, I have no doubts that you will get an A—but please find my comments in red," my Opa replied.

I was not always a good writer or even a good student. My teachers in Canada had made me feel small, insignificant, and unremarkable. I devoted years of mental growth and a steadfast commitment to my future professional goals to develop a level of confidence in my academic abilities. So, receiving words of encouragement like this was meaningful, especially from two loved ones I had always respected for their academic and professional brilliance.

It was too late to drop the course, but from that day forward, I did not attend a single class meeting, and obviously, I received an "F" overall. To make matters worse, my academic counselor advised me that Dr. Somma was practically unavoidable if I were going to major in political science, so I decided to switch to Criminology, specializing in Forensic Behavioral Science, to give myself a better chance for academic success.

Dr. Somma is not a stupid person; he is a tenured professor with a PhD. He is a smart man who is used to being right, but he was profoundly wrong that day. Handing in a well-written paper was not nearly enough. He still did not see me. He still did not see me for who I was and who I had the potential to become. He saw me only in the most superficial sense: he saw my outward appearance, the color of my skin, and my tardiness on the first day of class. As a nineteen-year-old college kid, I was overwhelmed by the prospect of having to prove him wrong about me and to force him to confront his biases, and unfortunately, I didn't try.

Regardless of whether it was intentional or unconscious, Dr. Somma held biases against me as an individual. But that was only one of the biases I was up against. He probably held negative views about people with tattoos and about student athletes. It did not really matter what biases he harbored. I felt like there was nothing I could do to remedy the situation. I felt completely powerless. *Why does this guy hate me so much?* The question kept running through my mind. To make sense of the encounter internally, I reasoned that *his* racism was *his* problem, and it was not my responsibility to "overcome" *his* bias in the first place.

COMPASSION

The perturbing experience I had with Dr. Somma, as well as the decision I made in response to it, burned in my mind for months. I decided to quit. I decided to take the loss, regroup, and move on. Perhaps my initial reaction was reasonable, but this approach to bias is not a sustainable solution in the long run.

I concluded that there must be a better way because my experience with Dr. Somma would inevitably repeat itself with other professors. *I cannot simply give up and change majors every time I come across a teacher with biases*, I thought. That could never be feasible. So, the following semester, I decided to take on a new approach.

On the first day of class of the new semester, for every single course on my schedule, I planned to hang back at the end of class to speak to the professor one-on-one. There would typically be a handful of other students with the same idea, so I would go to the back of the line. It was key that this conversation happened only between the professor and me. I wanted to create a safe environment. I needed the professor to feel comfortable having an honest and genuine conversation.

I vividly remember that first day of class, a Thursday, because it changed the course of my life. It was Criminology 101 with Dr. Candice Skrapec, another tenured, highly respected Fresno State University professor. This time, I had carefully thought out what I would say. I would not be caught off guard again. I had a plan.

I took a deep breath, and I said the following: "Hi Professor Skrapec, my name is Braeden Anderson. It is a pleasure to meet you and to be in your class. If you still have a few minutes, I really wanted to share a few quick thoughts."

"As you may have guessed by my height, I'm on the basketball team [pause and smile]. Unfortunately, as I'm sure you know, my travel and practice schedule can present some difficulties. I will have to miss class regularly, and sometimes it will be hard for me to keep up. First and foremost, I just want to express my gratitude in advance. I'm not sure what kind of experience you have had with student athletes in the past, but I know that you do not get paid any extra for having to accommodate my crazy basketball schedule. I know that allowing me to make up quizzes, tests, homework, and assignments can be a huge pain—and I just wanted you to know that I truly appreciate it, and I do not take you or this class for granted.

"I want to be a lawyer one day, I take my grades very seriously, and I really value my education. I am majoring in forensic behavioral science, and I was really excited to take this class with you because of your vast experience researching psychopathy and serial murderers. I also read that you have worked with law enforcement to assist in solving active and 'cold' criminal cases, which I found very interesting."

As I uttered this speech, I watched Dr. Skrapec's face soften with compassion and understanding before my eyes. She expressed her sincere appreciation that I took the time to speak with her and engaged me in conversation. She asked me a half-dozen questions about my background, about basketball, and about what I wanted to accomplish professionally. She gave me encouraging advice and assured me that we would work together to manage my basketball schedule. She saw me. Truly saw me. She saw me as someone with promise. Someone with potential. Someone who might become somebody one day. Someone smart. Someone worthy of teaching and perhaps even mentoring. After chatting with her for maybe fifteen minutes, I finally left the classroom, holding back tears of pure joy. I had done it! My plan had worked! What happened on that Thursday morning in the spring of 2013 would forever change the way I saw the world and other people. It would forever change the way I saw myself. And perhaps most importantly, it would forever change my strategy for navigating bias and racism.

Could it really be possible? I thought. *Is there some strange, magical power in reaching out to bridge the gap?* I repeated my speech four more times that week with my other professors, and each time I employed this proactive strategy, it invoked the same response. Each time, the professor was visibly relieved by my words. Relief was not the emotion I expected to witness, but it is the only accurate way to describe the phenomenon. They would sigh, almost imperceptibly, sport a warm smile, nod attentively, thank me sincerely, and from that moment forward, take a serious interest in both who I already was and who I was on a journey to become.

This markedly different reaction to my proactive approach made me further reflect on my fateful experience with Dr. Somma and other encounters with literally dozens of other teachers or authority figures before him who had similarly failed to "see" me. I began to believe in the capacity of each of these individuals to be visibly, genuinely touched by my words and rethink any initial negative opinions of me they might have formed based on my appearance. Relieved of their potential for racism. Relieved of their potential for bias. Relieved of their potential prejudices. Relieved of their potential predisposition to dislike me, treat me poorly, and underestimate me. Relieved of their problem.

Am I saying that every single one of my professors would have failed me as Dr. Somma did had I not proactively given them a speech to subversively help them confront their bias? No, not quite. I don't have enough evidence to draw that conclusion. My stories, no matter how inspiring they may be, amount to mere anecdotal evidence. But what I can say, with certainty, is that for thirteen years, I did not employ this technique, and I failed miserably to impress my true identity upon those around me. And giving this two-minute speech changed my life. It radically changed the way my professors treated me. The repeated success of such a seemingly simple tactic felt like discovering fire or like seeing the ocean for the very first time. I was absolutely blown away. A short, heartfelt conversation dismantled unconscious bias right before my eyes, right before it even had a chance to rear its ugly head.

In short, my proactive strategy harnessed and wielded a powerful weapon: compassion. This unassuming ingredient, if used properly, has the potential to obliterate unconscious bias. Generally, employing compassion as a strategy for overcoming adversity is not all that groundbreaking. But directing our empathy and compassion toward those we understandably view as "undeserving" of it likely does not come naturally for most people. It certainly did not for me.

It is a hard lesson to learn that not only are the kindest among us deserving of our compassion. Paradoxically, it is precisely when we are treated cruelly or unfairly by someone that the need to employ compassion is most dire. Compassion must dominate our mind's conscious intentions. We must not allow ourselves to be blinded by rage or by hurt. Compassion helps us understand how others are feeling so that we can respond appropriately to the situation. It is the brightly burning torch that lights the way along the path to discovering a haven of mutual understanding with others. Compassion reveals to us the true identity of another person; most importantly, it enables us to effectively influence others to see us for who we are rather than who we appear to be.

Employing tactful empathy with the specific purpose of achieving personal goals and defeating the bias of others is a form of behavioral manipulation. Using this technique would undoubtedly be unethical if we intended to cause harm to or deceive others, but we aim to do nothing of the sort. We are fighting to overcome

400 years of racism, and goddammit, we need to pull out the big guns. Tactful empathy is making calculated adjustments to our behavior with the knowledge that doing so will likely cause a particular and intended emotional or physical reaction in another person. Put simply, if we learn to understand precisely how bias operates in the human mind, we can adjust our actions and behavior to conquer it. When we employ tactful empathy in response to known factors that contribute to a person's biases, we can more accurately make predictions about which methods are most likely to result in achieving our goals in a world that desperately wants us to fall short of the mark.

Compassion can be used as a tool to foster unity. But compassion must be thoughtfully considered and carefully managed because it can also inhibit socially inclusive behavior and, consequently, breed divisiveness. For example, the instinctual compassion we feel for the plights of members of our family, social circle, or ethnic group may unintentionally spur the growth of bias against others, "outsiders" whom we perceive as posing a potential threat. The feeling of animosity toward a person who is not "one of us," whether conscious or unconscious, is completely normal. Human beings have evolved and survived, at least in part, because of our advanced protective instincts. We maneuver through life, gauging empathy levels to discern friends from foes, and sizing up the competition.

My professors had instinctive compassion for the students they perceived as the most like them. In years and years of teaching, they developed a keen sense of those characteristics that made a good student—how a good student behaved, dressed, spoke, and spent her time outside of class. They also developed a keen instinct about what made a "poor" student—those they did not understand, those with whom they did not empathize, and those who were unlikely to succeed.

My professors did not naturally have compassion for Black basketball players with tattoos. Black basketball players with tattoos who rarely were able to attend class. Black basketball players with tattoos who—when they did attend class—showed up late, wearing sweaty basketball shorts. Our professors did not see any of us as students. Our professors did not see us as being part of their social or ethnic circles. Our professors judged us based on our appearance, but they did not *see* us. Because of course, looks can be deceiving, and our innate sense of what separates "us" from "them" often miscalculates the truth. Being Black is not synonymous with being a threat. Being a basketball player is not synonymous with being a bad student. Having tattoos does not make one a criminal.

EMOTIONAL INTELLIGENCE

Sometimes, in order to be seen, we need to turn on the lights. Sometimes, in order to be treated as equals, we need to explain who we are and force others to check their assumptions at the door. Sometimes, in order to win the empathy of others, we need to prove that we are worthy of it. And sometimes, coming to terms with this unfortunate reality—that we must be the ones to put in the work to bridge the gap in understanding between "us" and "them"—requires emotional intelligence.

Daryl Davis is an activist and blues pianist from Chicago, Illinois. Daryl is also a Black man. Beginning in the 1980s, against all odds, he successfully convinced more than fifty active members of the KKK to abandon their iniquitous belief systems and denounce their KKK membership. One evening in 1983, Daryl was performing at a "white" bar in Frederick, Maryland, when he was approached by a white patron who complimented him on performance. The two sat down together, and the white patron eventually admitted that he was an active member of the KKK. The two developed a friendship, and the man gave Daryl the contact information of several Klan leaders at his request. Daryl was hated by the Klan because of his blackness, yet he befriended them. He was afraid of them, yet he chose to set aside his fear and study them. As these Klansmen spent time getting to know Daryl Davis, despite his blackness, they began to empathize with him and reconsider their own misconceptions about Black men. As mutual understanding between the parties grew, there was eventually no room for these men's racist attitudes. Daryl's story represents what is possible through cultivating emotional intelligence. His story reminds us that using tact is critical to conquering and overcoming racist ideas.

Emotional intelligence, as you may know, refers to a person's capacity to perceive, identify, and manage both her own emotions and the emotions of others. This ability can be further segmented into two main skills: emotional recognition and emotional diplomacy. Emotional recognition is essential to objectively analyzing the way we feel and consciously evaluating the meaning and root of those feelings. It is in the process of achieving thorough emotional understanding of ourselves that we become equipped to direct, harness, and mitigate those emotions. Remaining in touch with the emotional signals from within consciousness and those invoked in reaction to our environment makes us better spouses, parents, leaders, friends, and employees.

Racism stirs up a variety of powerful emotions in both its perpetrators and its victims. Not being seen by my professor made me feel small. It made me feel powerless. It made me feel like quitting, and at first, I did. But feelings are not facts, and I realized that I was not small (literally or figuratively). I was not powerless, and I would never again quit. I realized that what others think of me in any given moment is fleeting. I discovered that I am not defined by their views, and those opinions have the propensity to change over time. Mastering the ability to think objectively about how others thought about me drastically shifted my focus from self-pity and learned helplessness to a growth mentality: a commitment to relentlessly proving those who doubted me wrong. Exercising emotional diplomacy is the pinnacle of this ability. It involves using our knowledge of human behavioral science to solve problems and tactically navigate the emotions of others. Tactful emotional intelligence. This tool is critical to succeeding while black.

SELF-AWARENESS

It's a fact, albeit an unfortunate one, that harboring implicit biases is part of being human. We are imperfect creatures. Our ideas and opinions are a reflection of subjective influences melded from our unique upbringings, family values, levels of education, and socioeconomic status. Thus, humans are apt to make assumptions about people and circumstances based on what we have seen and experienced. As we know all too well, these assumptions are rarely grounded in fact and are often incorrect. Having intimate knowledge of our own biases is the first step to checking them.

When you fly on an airplane, the flight attendant instructs you to "Put on your own oxygen mask first" before helping others. If you run out of oxygen yourself, how can you help anyone else survive the calamity? The first step toward mastering a tactful approach to helping others overcome their bias is to acknowledge and face down our own.

When I went to check the mail recently, I crossed paths with a young woman pushing a baby stroller. This picture immediately evoked myriad split-second assumptions about her in my mind. It was 2:00 p.m., so I assumed she was unemployed. She was a young woman caring for a child, so I assumed the child was hers. I did not believe these assumptions were negative. They were just the truth, right? Wrong. After engaging her in conversation, I learned that she was gainfully employed as an engineer, the child was her niece, and she had taken the day off from work to help out because her sister was not feeling well. Luckily, in this case, my inaccurate pre-judgment was inconsequential, but unfortunately, assumptions often have an infinite capacity to cause harm. Experiences like this one impress upon us that regardless of how a person or circumstance may appear, making assumptions based solely on what is visible is a dangerous habit. We must check our affinity for quick judgment at the door.

The way a relationship begins does not determine how it will evolve in the future. Initial perceptions can be wildly inaccurate, but that fact does not control your destiny. As we get to know someone better, we gather more information with which to form an opinion. Over time, the veracity of our perceptions becomes more likely. When we look inward first and closely examine our own assumptions, we can identify what possible triggers have the potential to contribute to our exhibition of prejudicial behavior.

Learning to precisely predict when, why, and under what circumstances others may misunderstand us is like having the answers before test day. Self-awareness equips us with the ability to actively manage, mitigate, or avoid bias in the course of dismantling impediments to our professional success, whether they may be social or systemic.

I have tattoos covering both shoulders and biceps, my right forearm, and my right wrist—amounting to a full sleeve on my right arm and a half-sleeve on the other. I also have tattoos on my chest and left calf. It has been highly uncommon for me to encounter other attorneys with a level of visible tattoo coverage comparable to mine. Did my tattoos make me a less capable student? Does having tattoos inherently make me unprofessional in my practice? More likely to be a criminal? Of course, the answer to each of these questions is no, but for many, my tattoos automatically invoke those stereotypes. To a self-aware person, the knowledge that these stereotypes about individuals (more specifically, Black men) with tattoos are prevalent is the key fact. Maintaining awareness that there is a risk of being stigmatized merely because of my tattoos has granted me the power to chart a course capable of circumventing discrimination on this fact alone.

What do I do with this kind of information once I recognize it and mentally file it away? What do I do with what I learn from studying the behavior of others? The answers to these questions are not so straightforward. While I acknowledge that having tattoos may increase my risk of stigmatization, I do not regret my choice to get a single one. Regretting characteristics that may subject you to discrimination is not a virtue. I do not regret my tattoos, just as I do not regret my blackness.

Each of my tattoos has deep, personal meaning— and they collectively depict an artful expression of who I was yesterday, who I am today, and who I want to be tomorrow. But as a person who has tattoos, I am biased too. I feel justified in my belief that having tattoos, even in a professional environment, is perfectly fine. And I feel compelled to chastise those who judge me for it. After all, the truth about me defies any stereotypes: I am a lawyer, I am not a criminal, and I was a good student.

With that said, I must acknowledge and be willing to accept that reasonable minds could disagree with my position. My professors could disagree. My boss could disagree. Many good people who could add value to my life might disagree. Because of my awareness of these facts, during most workdays, job interviews, and occasions where I may meet someone new, I am careful to wear long sleeves and a watch on my right wrist to keep my tattoos covered. My choice to cover up typically allows for an opportunity to effectively express who I am and make a positive first impression before others have the chance to stereotype me.

We cannot safely rely on being afforded the benefit of the doubt. The influential people in our personal and professional lives must see the truth about who we are. We must be patient, and we must accept that not everyone we meet will initially grasp the plenitude of our identity. We have to be willing to extend our hand and demonstrate our true worth to others, even if we hate that we have to. We must be self-aware of how our "vulnerabilities" may be perceived, regardless of the way we perceive ourselves.

When we meet someone for the first time, we have very little information with which to make an informed judgement call about them, yet the human brain is still programmed to try. Self-awareness allows us to approach new acquaintances with compassion and kindness—despite their flaws and prejudices. Self-awareness forces us to see human beings as human beings, each of us beautiful, brimming with imperfections. The way others react or treat me because of my height, my weight, my gender, my race, or my tattoos is entirely outside of my control. Self-awareness helps us make peace with the frustration and anger we feel when faced with the bias of others and instead focus on how we will react. We must seize the opportunity to adjust our own behavior to head off bias before it presents itself.

Without giving my professors a speech, they may not have believed in my potential as a student. But so what? They did believe. Without wearing long sleeves and my watch on the wrong wrist, I may not have been hired. But who cares? I was hired.

As a lawyer, I meet important people every day. Sometimes they are clients. Sometimes they are colleagues. Sometimes they are supervisors. But always, they are important. These people are important to me and to my future success. But sometimes, these individuals do not immediately see me as important to them and to their future success. As Black people, we know this experience and the chagrin it invokes all too well. Sometimes, social rejection involves very subtle behavior—as subtle as someone not making eye contact with us, not introducing themselves, not asking us any questions about ourselves, or merely appearing disinterested. Other times, it feels more intentional and personal—as intentional and personal as not offering us the job, no matter how qualified we are; not promoting us when we have clearly earned it above our peers; or not allowing us to keep our lives after being stopped by police. Regardless of the form in which it manifests or its impact on its victims, experiencing racism is like being in the belly of the beast.

Whether the problem is overcoming bias in America, slowing global warming, or figuring out how to make rent in New York City, we must thoughtfully and analytically devise a solution to the identified problem. In order to combat racism at school, at work, and in the game of life, we must be thoughtful. The decisions we make each day determine our future. And we need to make good ones. Letting go of our inability to change the behavior of others and shifting our focus inward allows us to think objectively and direct our mental energy toward factors that are within our control.

In tackling a problem, I methodically follow these four steps and repeat as many times as needed:

1. Assess the quality and relevance of available information;
2. Analyze the useful data you identified;
3. Form a conclusion that the analysis of your data supports;
4. Consider the big picture and acknowledge other perspectives.

Following these four steps raises important questions along the way. Is there any clear evidence of bias in the situation in which I find myself? Would it be reasonable to assume that implicit bias is likely present? Is there any harm in assuming that this person may hold biases against me? What conclusions should I draw based on the answers to these questions? What are some alternative theories? If I reach the conclusion that bias is negatively influencing someone's opinion of me, what should I do about it? Is it worth it? Is this person important to my life? Could this person's bias be permanently damaging to my future prospects?

The process of thinking through the answers to these questions will instill us with confidence in our ability to solve the problems we encounter in our daily lives, whether related to race or something else. But gathering information and reaching correct conclusions is not the final ingredient. Effectively using tact to overcome bias still requires one last element.

DIPLOMACY

This skill is the most critical to persuasive communication, and employing it appropriately often fosters mutual respect. The art of diplomacy involves asserting your ideas or opinions in a manner that does not damage the relationship or offend. David Frost famously wrote, "Diplomacy is the art of letting somebody else have your way."

So, you suspect that your boss may be racist. Or perhaps, she has explicitly made a racist comment in the course of a workplace conversation. But now what? Determining the manner in which to respond, choosing a course of action that will not permanently damage your future professional prospects, is a difficult process.

Let's think about the situation you find yourself in a little differently. Instead of saying to yourself, *My boss is racist*, reframe this conclusion to, *My boss does not yet fully understand who I am or what I am capable of.* While you may feel compelled to explicitly call out your boss for her racist statement, that's not likely the smartest course. Rather, the most effective response may be to simply withhold your opinion of her behavior and allow her to stumble over herself to quickly save face.

Commonly, racism in the workplace takes the subtle form of not being as valued by your superiors as your white peers; not being respected by your colleagues; not being considered by management for the best opportunities; and not being recognized for your accomplishments. How should you confront these subtleties? Perhaps you should boldly express yourself, clearly etching out your professional goals and how you intend to achieve them. Or perhaps, you may find it beneficial to introduce your perspectives more quietly, allowing the other person to feel as though they have reached your conclusion on their own.

As a Black basketball player with tattoos, I learned to accept and proactively head off my professors' propensity for harboring bias against me. As Black people, we must employ the same strategy to address bias in the workplace. Bias can be as resounding and conspicuous as a gunshot or as quiet and mysterious as being laid off. Hidden or apparent, you will not escape it. But if we can accept this fact, we can learn to identify it, plan for it, and defeat it.

CHAPTER 5

RAD REFUSE TO ACCEPT DEFEAT

SUPPOSE YOU ARE A BRILLIANT, powerful Black woman, and you run as the Democratic candidate for governor of Georgia in the 2018 election, becoming the first Black female major-party gubernatorial nominee in the United States. Suppose that, as many (and I'm one of them) believe, voter suppression occurs, and you lose. What do you do? Do you tuck your tail and go home? Do you accept that the rules are rigged against you, and there's nothing you can do to change them? Do you react as I did after my professor accused me of cheating and quit? Not if you're Stacey Abrams. Here's what she did:

In 2019, she became the first Black woman to deliver a response to the State of the Union Address. Despite encouragement from many stakeholders and constituents to seek election to senatorial seats in her state, she chose instead to focus her energy on fighting voter suppression. To that end, she founded Fair Fight 2020, an organization created with the goal of assisting Democrats financially and technically to build voter protection teams in twenty states. As part of the 2020 presidential election, Abrams served as an elector for the state of Georgia. She is credited by both *The New York Times* and *The Washington Post* for an estimated 800,000 new voter registrations, boosting Georgia's Democratic voter turnout in the 2020 presidential election—where Joe Biden won the state—and in Georgia's 2020–21 U.S. Senate elections and special elections, which gave Democrats control over the Senate.

That's what winning looks like. To put it in the words of Stacey Abrams, "When people doubt your right to be somewhere, the responsibility falls on you to prove over and over again that you deserve to be there."

This statement packs a punch and clearly articulates something that is often difficult for Black folks to acknowledge. The responsibility falls on us. The rules of the game have been set. If we do not like them, it is our responsibility to see that they are changed. If we cannot change them, it is our responsibility to succeed despite them. It is imperative that we remember this and that we follow her example.

Stacey Abrams isn't just a name in a history book—although, believe me, she will be one day, and what a history book it will be. She's a living, breathing, amazing success story we get to witness in real time. Just as important, she is the most perfect example I can imagine of manifesting the mantra: Refuse to Accept Defeat.

I don't have to explain to the Black colleagues and students I mentor why I talk about defeat before I talk about success. As you saw in the previous chapters, defeat came before success in my life, and it probably did in yours, too. Losing is frustrating, but it's temporary and provisional. Losses must be categorically studied, learned from, and forcefully avoided in the future.

THE DEEP END

Retired Navy SEAL David Goggins is the only member of the U.S. Armed Forces to complete SEAL training, graduate from the U.S. Army Ranger School as an Enlisted "Honor Man," and finish Air Force Tactical Air Controller training. He's also completed more than sixty ultra-marathons, triathlons, and ultra-triathlons, setting new course records, and regularly placing in the top five. He once held the Guinness World Record for pull-ups, having completed 4,030 in seventeen hours. But that's not where he started. He started where a lot of us did, poor and abused. Add to that obesity, asthma, a congenital heart defect—and of course, racism. But Goggins developed a valuable mindset—the 40 percent rule. That is, "When your mind is telling you you're done, you're only 40 percent done." This rule and his own motivation pushed him ahead when others would have quit.

You, of course, have your own problems and challenges. Life is difficult enough without the added stress and struggle of facing racism. Many hardships I endured were a result of being raised in an abusive household. Some hardships stemmed from my family's lack of financial support and my lack of a dependable male role model to guide me. Others, such as breaking my neck in a horrific car crash, might just be bad luck.

But I promise you, we are built for this. Our genetic architecture has evolved to triumph over adversity, and we are resilient beyond articulation. This inherent power cannot be stolen from us. It was earned by those who came before us. It was bought and paid for by our Black ancestors who fought for every inch of freedom that we now enjoy. The war is not over, however, and we are ordained with the duty to use our innate resilience to vigorously continue the fight.

This fight begins and ends with practicing RAD— and refusing to accept defeat. Let me explain.

Despite the obstacles we have endured, nothing can truly stop us unless we accept defeat. Nothing can stop us unless we quit. I implore you to never accept a fate that amounts to less than what you dream you can achieve. RAD begins with a profound threshold question: What future do I want for myself? It is important that you first answer this question with as much specificity and detail as possible. Your answer to this question will be your lighthouse on every stormy day, a shining light that will guide your ship as you traverse the treacherous obstacles along your journey.

Here is how I answered that question. I decided when I was maybe fourteen years old that I was destined to be successful in life. I decided that I was a scholar and an athlete. I decided that I would use the game of basketball as a vehicle to take me out of my troubled circumstances. I decided that I would use basketball to earn a college education and then leverage that education to become either a doctor or a lawyer. Period. This was what success would look like for me. Anything less would not suffice. Making it to the NBA or becoming a doctor or a lawyer was the future I saw and expected for myself, and I promised myself that I would refuse to accept anything less. It did not matter what other people thought. It did not matter what other people did to me or said to me. It did not matter if they tried to stop me.

Like most Black children, I experienced racism at an early age. Yet, racism isn't like a gunshot; it's more like a hammer trying to beat you into the ground. You feel each blow, but you don't immediately connect the pain of the current one to those that came before it. The power of the hammer is augmented or weakened by the love and support you are or are not receiving at home.

When I was eleven, my maternal grandmother (whom I called "Nana") gave me a new bike for my birthday. For weeks, I rode that cherished bike to basketball practice and carefully parked it at the racks. One day, as I was locking it up, I saw a group of white guys eyeing me, but I was in a hurry, so I ignored them and went inside. When I returned after practice, my bike was a heap of metal and rubber, totally destroyed. The tires were flat. The wheels were bent. The spokes were snapped and twisted. The dented frame—ironically still locked to the rack—lay on the ground, engraved, in capital letters, with the word "NIGGER."

That same year, I was on a winter camping trip with the Boy Scouts program. Several other boys and I were having an against-the-rules snowball fight. The fun was put to an end when the group scout master eventually caught us. He was not impressed and approached us in a manner that reflected the same.

At least eight of us were participating in the illicit snowball throwing, but he pointed at me.

"Braeden," he said. "Come here, boy, now."

I walked over, confused as to why I was the only one he called.

"If I have to talk to you again," he said, "you are not going to like the consequences."

"Why am I the only one who's in trouble?" I asked him.

I'll never forget his next words.

"You stand out in a crowd."

Later that day, we were playing two-hand-touch football in the snow when a bulky kid, four years my senior, shoved me to the ground.

"Hey, fuck you," I said.

"What're you going to do about it, nigger?"

Naturally, a fight ensued. I hit him in the face, and the other guys had to pull us apart. As a punishment for my "second offense," the group scout master forced me to shovel snow off of nearby dirt walkways and a twenty-five-flight metal outdoor staircase.

Yet, I won.

I won because I mentally drowned out his voice and the voices of all of those who doubted me. I won because my battles and even my defeats made me stronger. I won because right now, as I write this book after a cold, hard winter for our nation and our world, and regardless of the challenges I'm facing, I am living my best life.

Racism is like being thrown in the deep end of the pool and learning how to swim. No one's going to be able to prepare you for what it's like. No one's going to be able to get to you quick enough to save you if you sink. You need a plan.

If you come equipped, even if you are pushed into the deep end, you can be your own life preserver. To quote David Goggins, "There are valuable lessons to learn in the deep end! Life is the most unexpected thing you will ever encounter. It loves taking you to the deep end just to see if you can fucking swim! Stay hard!"

NO DRAMA

When I first heard about Barack Obama, I was thirteen years old, and I thought I'd already figured out how the world worked...my world anyway. Here was this Black guy running for president, and I felt almost sad because I knew he really deserved it and that he could do it if he just had a chance. But a Black president in America? Yeah, right. Yet, as he continued to push forward, I started asking myself: Could he really do it? Was it really possible? And what about racism?

Barack Obama becoming President of the United States gave me hope—very simple, very subtle hope. It didn't tell me there wasn't racism in America because there is. It didn't massage away all my fears because they're real. It didn't help that Obama was battling those same injustices and challenges that I was and that the entire Black community was, too. What mattered was the way he shouldered it all with such grace and such dignity that prejudices almost melted away.

Obama's greatness is undeniable. As I witnessed it, I was astonished, almost in disbelief. In the inauguration, in the swearing in. A Black family had actually moved into the White House. The whole time, I was on the edge of my seat, afraid something was going to happen, and my hope was going to slip away. But it didn't. 43 white male presidents before him over nearly 220 years. Finally, I thought, the reason I can't become president of the United States is not because I'm Black; it's because I'm Canadian. That was much easier to accept. I could always run for Congress.

"Change will not come if we wait for some other person or some other time," President Obama said. "We are the ones we've been waiting for. We are the change we seek."

Despite the credit that has been given to him, it's not enough. A guy from Hawaii, son of parents from Kenya and Kansas, who grew up without his biological father, excelling at basketball, graduating magna cum laude from Harvard Law, becoming the first Black editor of *the Harvard Law Review*—he was and is the ultimate American success story.

. His 2015 singing of "Amazing Grace" during the eulogy for Rev. Clementa Pinckney, who was killed the previous month in a shooting at a Charleston church, was widely acknowledged as one of the most powerful moments of his presidency.

He faced indignities, lies, racism, crazy birther conspiracies, and name-calling, yet he was cool, a master at tactful empathy. "No-Drama Obama" he was nicknamed by both those who admired his style and those who didn't.

We live in an imperfect world, but it's a world where Barack Obama's journey is possible.

"I have an even temperament and I don't get too high and I don't get too low, but that doesn't mean that throughout the presidency and throughout my professional career that there weren't times when I was constrained by, 'Man I don't want to screw this up. I don't want to let people down,'" he said at a conference hosted by software company Qualtrics in 2019. "'I don't want to be seen as having made a mistake or having failed.'"[3]

3   Harvard, Sarah. "How to stay cool under pressure, according to Barack Obama," *The Independent*, March 11, 2019, https://www.independent.co.uk/news/world/americas/us-politics/barack-obama-how-to-stay-calm-under-pressure-cool-advice-tips-a8818046.html.

CONFIRMATION BIAS

Part of the difficulty in overcoming bias of any kind, especially confirmation bias, is the way that it can alter or cloud your perception of yourself. Racist people want you to behave as they perceive a Black person behaves. Depending on the situation or context, someone may perceive you to have a certain disposition for a particular emotion or pervasive personality trait, such as anger, arrogance, or ignorance. Other times, these false perceptions are rooted in stereotypes about Black careers, talents, or skills. For example, there are certain things white people think we *can* do. These things generally include bouncing or throwing various round objects, dribbling, shooting, and running with said objects very fast, on fields, on courts, or on tracks. All too often the fact that we can also proficiently read, write, think critically, lead and manage, analyze, and negotiate is more difficult to accept.

This gap in understanding and appreciation between perception and reality is where the problem lies. Certain people, as brave as they may be, avoid this sticky, difficult place, and they drift toward the margins. They avoid conflict, big dreams, big goals, big jobs. Others—and you can be one of them—gravitate toward their goals in the midst of chaos, keep calm, and keep keeping on. No drama. Everything is cool.

Take Kamala Harris, who is a prominent member of the group that receives the vilest online attacks from internet trolls—female politicians. As I write this book in the early months of the Biden/Harris administration, research shows that Kamala Harris may be the most targeted American politician on the internet, one who, according to the *Los Angeles Times*, "checks every box for the haters of the fever swamps: She's a woman, she's a person of color, and she holds power."[4]

Unlike the Biden haters, who call him creepy or sleepy in deference to their former president, the Harris haters concoct conspiracies alleging that she wielded sex as a weapon to get to the top and that she therefore doesn't deserve her office or the power that comes with it. As I write this, at least one recent study suggests that American female politicians are two to three times more likely than male politicians to receive abusive Twitter comments.[5]

Nina Jankowicz, a fellow at the Wilson Center, led a 2021 study that analyzed more than 300,000 posts in the several months leading up to the 2020 U.S. presidential election. Harris was targeted in 78 percent—more than

---

4   Bierman, Noah. "Black, female and high-profile, Kamala Harris is a top target in online fever swamps," *Los Angeles Times*, February 19, 2021, www.latimes.com.

5   Guerin, Cecile and Eisha Maharasingam-Shah. "Public Figures, Public Rage: Candidate abuse on social media," *Institute for Strategic Dialogue*, October 5, 2020, isdglobal.org.

any other high-profile women of color.[6] Here's something that should surprise you but probably won't: the attacks and lies attempting to smear Harris had something in common with the lies that were used in attempts to denigrate Barack and Michelle Obama.

Those lies fell into the following categories:

The other/illegal. Because of her mixed-race heritage (sound familiar?), Harris cannot legally serve as vice president.

A secret agenda. She's the one with the real power; Biden is just a clueless figurehead.

These comments speak volumes about the people spreading and actually believing the lies. They fear a powerful woman of color so much that they will convince themselves and try to convince others that she's something other than she appears, because how could a person of color be the real deal? How could a little girl from Oakland, California, have the audacity to go to law school and to become Attorney General of California, and then the second African American woman and the first South Asian American to serve in the United States Senate, let alone be elected to the second-highest office in the land? Kamala Harris did it. And while

---

6   Nina Jankowicz et al. "Malign Creativity: How Gender, Sex, and Lies are Weaponized against Women Online," *Wilson Center*, January 2021, wilsoncenter.org.

people were talking about her Chuck Taylors (because when a woman runs for office, you've got to talk about her fashion choices), she wore those shoes all the way to the White House.

When you're in that no-drama zone, your thoughts go something like this: *Your false perceptions of who I am won't define me. Your ideas about me are fiction, and they don't scare me.* They didn't scare Kamala Harris, who made history with her election to vice president. And they didn't scare Barack Obama, who proved that one of us could run for the highest political office in the United States and win.

That's what's possible in the United States of America. Racists want you to have a war. Racists want you to burn down buildings so they can kill you and believe confirmation bias that can justify their negative feelings about you. They want drama. They want you to get frustrated, to lose your cool, to quit, or better yet, to not even try.

In 2016, when I applied to the law firm where I started my career, I knew that both Barack and Michelle Obama had worked there, and I wanted to be there too. It was encouraging to me that two Black people whom I admired had walked the path before me and succeeded. They had succeeded at a law firm which was founded in 1866 and had a 150-year history of excellence in the practice of law. Their success captivated me.

YOU ARE RESILIENT

Resilient people do not search for excuses. They search for solutions. Resilient people take responsibility for their own success. They have a winning daily routine and stay laser-focused on their purpose. Resilient people set specific goals and obsessively scheme about how to achieve them. They approach each new day with a beginner's mind, and they are eager to learn. Resilient people do not fear risk; they accept risk. They do not fear failure; they fear accepting failure.

WE CAN WIN EVEN WHEN WE FAIL

Life is not fair. We cannot choose our starting line in life, but present circumstances need not dictate our future. What happens to us is often not within our control, but the decisions we make control a whole lot. All that matters is how you play the game and whether you win or lose. The more adversity we face on our journey to reaching a goal, the sweeter the victory is.

James Baldwin said, "Not everything can be changed, but nothing can be changed until it is faced."

Recognizing the distinction between resilience and accepting defeat should be considered virtuous, not vilifying. The heart of this distinction lies not in the level of success you have already achieved but in the attitude and appetite with which you approach daily life. Resilience is a mentality. So is accepting defeat. We can choose to allow our minds to be dominated by regret, fear, excuses, and self-doubt. Or we can choose positivity; we can decide to execute on each and every variable within our control, over and over again, until the universe is compelled to bear its treasured fruit.

ASK YOURSELF

Winning begins with self-confidence. If you do not believe in yourself, how can anyone else? Do you value yourself and feel worthy of achieving massive success? Confidence is a tool, a tool capable of systematically invalidating our own insecurities and capable of providing us with total immunity to the negative opinions of others. Confidence attracts people, it attracts opportunities, and it inspires trust.

What is your unequivocal purpose?

One of the most important things you can do right now is set specific goals for yourself. Goals can be small (finishing an assignment) or large (going for a top job, writing a book) but each of them is your first step toward success.

Write down those goals. That gives you clarity and visualization on the things you want to achieve. The SMART method, commonly attributed to Peter Drucker, is also a valuable tool for success in planning goals for the future. The acronym SMART is commonly used to describe a useful goal.

Specific. Set a clearly defined simple goal.

Measurable. Make sure the goal is motivating but also something you can measure.

Achievable. Make sure the goal is attainable and something you can accomplish with effort.

Relevant. Make sure the goal is realistic, and results can be beneficial to your bigger goals.

Time-bound. Imagine all your goals are time sensitive, and you must achieve them quickly and efficiently to move on.

POSITIVE SELF-TALK

Tell yourself that what happened to you before had nothing to do with who you are. Tell yourself that you have the power to make changes, not wait for changes to be made. Tell yourself—and remind yourself—that a Black woman in Georgia lost an election and went on to play an instrumental role in electing the next American President.

I want to end this part of our conversation the way we started it: with Stacey Abrams. She said, "Don't let setbacks set you back."

We aren't about setbacks. We are about moving forward. We are about our goals, our accomplishments. So, tell me. What level of success are you willing to accept for yourself? What kind of life do you believe you deserve? What obstacles might stand in your way? The answers to these questions paint a vivid picture of the future.

CHAPTER 6

KNOWLEDGE IS BLACK POWER

THERE IS NO FORCE IN the universe more empowering to the Black community than education. No barrier to opportunity can effectively stand against it. Education is the great equalizer. It is the fundamental precondition for socioeconomic growth, democracy, and social justice. In elevating our minds academically, we can change the course of our family story, entrenching permanent advantages for all generations that come after us. Knowledge is power. Education brings not only knowledge but also proof of knowledge. A powerful credential signifying your right to participate in the economy. A powerful credential that is difficult to ignore and can never be taken from you. Education is not merely a key that opens doors but rather a bludgeon. A mighty bludgeon powerful enough to clobber, batter, and bash to the ground any door or obstacle with the nerve to stand in your way.

But as Black people, we historically have faced and will continue to face barriers to academic success; so will our children. This is not a secret, and there is no virtue in denial. We must accept the reality of racism and scheme against it. We must be thoughtful, crafty, and cunning. We must systematically plot to break down the barriers to education that have plagued our people in the same manner our oppressors systematically schemed to erect them in the first place. We must be ever conscious of the treacherous landscape that we are navigating as we strive for success. And with this awareness, remain committed to formulating a game plan to outwit and outmaneuver each disadvantage.

Black neighborhoods are more likely to have low quality schools, inadequate resources, and higher crime rates.[7] Without feelings of consistency, support, and safety, students are more likely to have lower grades—not because they are incapable of learning the material but simply because of the disadvantages of their circumstances. The correlation is even greater with students who move or change schools frequently.[8] Andrea Elliott, author of *Invisible Child*, describes that school

7   Tommy Shelby. *Dark Ghettos: Injustice, Dissent, and Reform* (Cambridge: Belknap Press, 2016).

8   Stacy M. Deck. "School outcomes for homeless children," *Journal of Children and Poverty* 23, no. 1 (2016): 4, doi: 10.1080/10796126.2016.1247347.

is not just a place to cultivate a hungry mind. School can be a refuge and can provide routine, nourishment, and guidance.

Since COVID-19, disparities between those with and without college degrees have been even more stark. According to Ingrid Gould Ellen, a professor of urban planning and a faculty director at the NYU Furman Center, those with college degrees had greater opportunities to work remotely and shelter in place. This puts less educated individuals at higher risk of contracting COVID-19, provides less flexibility for them to make up any hours they miss, and provides them with worse healthcare plans than the plans afforded to workers with degrees. We also saw that New York City neighborhoods with higher infection rates had a college graduate population of 29 percent, whereas neighborhoods with lower infection rates had a college graduate population of 47 percent.[9]

While most schools went online during COVID-19, that didn't mean that access to education was equal. From the 2018 Pew Research Center survey, black teens were less likely to have access to a computer or internet than their white peers. 25 percent of black teens did not

---

9   Erin Schumaker. "In NYC, 'stark contrast' in COVID-19 infection rates basedoneducationandrace,"*ABCNews*,April10,2020,https://abcnews. go.com/Health/nyc-stark-contrast-covid-19-infection-rates-based/ story?id=69920706.

have access to a computer with internet, versus only 13 percent of white teens.[10]

Data from the U.S. Department of Education shows that Black students are suspended and expelled at more than three times the rate of white students. Consequently, many of these Black students drop out of school completely. When these students drop out of school, they are much more likely to end up in the juvenile justice system. This pattern is referred to as the "school-to-prison pipeline."

It is not uncommon for teenage boys to grow into men while in prison, serving unimaginably long sentences. Reginald Dwayne Betts, a man who was incarcerated as a teenager and served a nine-year sentence, knew a prisoner who was sentenced to ninety years without parole as a teenager, whom he describes as "holding a clock with no hands."[11] And the pipeline starts early on in life.

Dr. Walter Gilliam from Yale University School of Medicine concluded that there are three factors that make a child more likely to be kicked out of preschool:

---

10   Anderson, Monica and Andrew Perrin. "Nearly one in five teens can't always finish their homework because of the digital divide," *Pew Research Center*, October 26, 2018, https://www.pewresearch.org/fact-tank/2018/10/26/nearly-one-in-five-teens-cant-always-finish-their-homework-because-of-the-digital-divide/.

11   Nicole R. Fleetwood. *Marking Time* (Cambridge: Harvard University Press, 2020).

being Black, being male, and looking older than his classmates.

With this frame of reference, you can imagine that school was tough for me. I was a gigantic Black boy who was expelled three times. Fortunately, I managed to escape the fate of landing in the pipeline. I had to fight endlessly to avoid the plight that befalls so many of us.

We have fought for a millennium for equal opportunity. We have made remarkable progress, but the fight must continue.

Obtaining a formal education and acquiring knowledge are two different things, but either can be a deadly weapon in an effort to destroy systemic racism. The failure to amass a fortune of knowledge is inexcusable. There are far fewer barriers to accessing knowledge than a formal education—especially today. Near-infinite amounts of information available free of charge to anyone who can afford Wi-Fi. Have a question? Explore, identify, and consume the millions of free data sources on the subject. The process of identifying quality information and deciphering between false and accurate information can be difficult. Without the necessary context or relevant background knowledge, it is easy to fall victim to fake news. Without a high school education, it may be difficult to determine what information can or should be trusted. Without a college education, it may be difficult to determine how to most efficiently select and leverage information. Obtaining a degree can make knowledge more valuable and provide more utility. Yet, not everyone has the opportunity to obtain a formal education. There are barriers.

At age fourteen, my English class was reading *To Kill a Mockingbird* by Harper Lee. My white classmates each took turns reading pages from the book aloud. Billy was reading when the word "nigger" made its first appearance. As the word left his lips, his eyes lit up with joy and amazement. He glanced around the room at his friends with a childish grin, as the other students softly chuckled. The word "nigger" appeared forty-seven more times in the book. Each time it appeared, my classmates visibly enjoyed reading or hearing the word. And forty-seven times, I grimaced and clenched my teeth as my heart ached with humiliation. Even though I protested having to sit through this novel, my teacher Mrs. Gerwien would not relent, insisting that I take part. She temporarily allowed me to substitute a different novel, but then rescinded and stated that this class was just "not for you." I was forced to drop the class.

At age fifteen, I was playing in a high school basketball game. It was an away game, and their school was in the "country," practically in the middle of nowhere. I was playing well, and we were winning. The opposing team quickly got frustrated that they couldn't stop me and started taking cheap shots at me. It started with some hard fouls and forceful pushing, but it escalated to one of the opposing team's players full-on tackling me while I was taking a shot. My head bounced violently off the gymnasium floor. I stumbled to my feet in dazed anger as I listened for a whistle that never came.

I looked over at the referee in astonishment and yelled, "Are you for real?"

As I ran back on defense, the player who tackled me shouted, "You're not getting shit. We don't like niggers around here."

I was over it. I pushed him to the ground and was soon brawling with all five opposing players. The referee blew his whistle, ejecting me from the game and ordering me to get the fuck out. I shoved open the double doors and exited the gym enraged, punching a glass picture frame on the wall in the process. When the principal of my high school heard about the incident, he suspended me for two weeks and forced me to handwrite letters of apology to the referees, the opposing school's administrators, all of their coaches, and all of their players. Despite my protests, no apology was ever offered to me.

It may not always feel like it, but with the right tools, you have the power over your life's trajectory. Howard

Bahr says that power represents survival.[12] When do we feel powerless? When do we feel at the mercy of others? It is when we don't have control over our surroundings, especially those that directly impact us. True power comes from control over the physical and social. It comes from affiliations, whether that be with larger institutions or with other influential people.

According to Amos H. Hawley, "Whatever power an individual might appear to possess is in effect attached to the office he occupies in a system."[13]

Education is one direct way to begin accumulating power and thus control over your life. Attending elite college, especially for people of color and those from disadvantaged backgrounds, is a social and economic mobility rocket. It automatically places you in an arena surrounded by the smartest and most connected network. You will have the opportunity to be taught by leaders of academic fields, conduct research with visionaries, and learn alongside the children of CEOs. After graduating, this network and the resources that come along with it only grow. In all corners of every industry and company, you will find leaders who are alumni of elite colleges and universities. However, only at the top

---

12   Howard Bahr. *Skid Row* (Oxford: Oxford University Press, 1973), 31.
13   Amos H. Hawley. "Community power and urban renewal success," *American Journal of Sociology* 68, no. 4 (1963): 423, doi: 10.1086/223399.

of every industry will these name brands be considered a requirement, the secret key needed to pass through the most exclusive and prestigious gates. Sociologist Lauren Rivera suggests in her studies that students from elite institutions are advantaged when applying for work in law, investment banking, and consulting.[14] If that isn't enough of an advantage, graduates from elite colleges had an income 39 percent higher than those from lower ranked public universities.[15]

But am I deserving of an elite college experience? Absolutely, yes. You have a powerful drive to succeed. It is your mission to show them this. Far too often, students from disadvantaged backgrounds "under-match." Stanford economist Caroline M. Hoxby uses this term to describe colleges which fail to reach their academic profile.[16] This results in elite colleges having fewer students from disadvantaged backgrounds, who then end up at community colleges or public universities. These educational institutions usually provide fewer resources, smaller financial aid packages, and have lower gradua-

14   Lauren A. Rivera. *Pedigree: How Elite Students Get Elite Jobs* (Princeton: Princeton University Press, 2016).

15   Anthony Abraham Jack. *The Privileged Poor* (Cambridge: Harvard University Press, 2019).

16   Hoxby, Caroline and Sarah Turner. "Expanding College Opportunities for High-Achieving, Low Income Students," *Stanford Institute for Economic Policy Research,* no. 12-014 (2013).

tion rates.[17] On average, elite colleges have a 90 percent or higher graduation rate compared to community colleges with a rate of 57 percent.[18] But despite these statistics, you can make a conscious decision to follow a different path.

Our education system is only beginning to realize that students from different backgrounds learn differently. Justine Cassell from Carnegie Mellon discovered that Black children learned science better when taught in African American Vernacular English.[19] Black children grow up with the unique experience of codeswitching between AAVE and Standard American English. Since elite America, including the educational and professional institutions it holds, communicates in Standard American English, Black children must learn to seamlessly switch between the two.

We oftentimes place too high of an importance on external validation and not enough on how we define ourselves. A study done on two groups of college students demonstrated how powerful external validation is in the school system. A group of A-students were given Ds while a group of D-students were given

17   Anthony Abraham Jack. *The Privileged Poor* (Cambridge: Harvard University Press, 2019).

18   Anthony Abraham Jack. *The Privileged Poor* (Cambridge: Harvard University Press, 2019).

19   Ruha Benjamin. *Race After Technology* (Cambridge: Polity, 2019), 180-181.

As, even though neither group deserved these grades. The results were astounding. The A-students started to produce D-level work while the D-students began to produce A-level work. Can you imagine the type of work you could produce, the amount of confidence you could exude, the potential success you could face if only you could channel that need for external validation inwards? This study not only shows the impact of external validation, but it also gives us an opportunity to see the unrealized power that our minds have over our own success. Because with unrelenting focus and drive, you are in complete control of your success.

Low-income Black students who attend elite college most often come from elite private high schools. The validation that comes from attending an elite school not only provides Black students with social and economic mobility resources sooner in life but also allows them to navigate the arena of the wealthy and elite. Anthony Abraham Jack calls this group of students the Privileged Poor. While I did not grow up with a stable family life or have access to many financial resources, my ability to bounce a basketball enabled me to gain access to wealthy and accomplished individuals. It enabled me to learn and grow. It enabled me to gain a formal education. It enabled me to leverage my talents in many areas, including networking. And eventually, it enabled me to secure a job practicing law for the largest law firm in the world (as of 2022).

I may have had slim odds of success as a once-home-less-teenage-high-school-dropout. But anyone who bet against me lost money.

With the right work ethic and the desire to pursue knowledge, you will gain full access to privilege. Never bet against yourself, and never bet against the power of education. We are all worthy of privilege. Do not envy those who appear to have privilege by virtue of their social status or the color of their skin. Those who earn their privilege keep it for good. Those who inherit their privilege are forever liable to lose it.

CHAPTER 7

SURVIVING THE POLICE

WHEN I WAS TWELVE YEARS old, I was skateboarding in my neighborhood and moving along at a pretty good pace when I was stopped by police.

"Why are you in such a hurry?" one of the officers asked.

"No reason," I said.

"Oh, really?" He studied me suspiciously. "Where do you live?"

I told him, and they reluctantly let me go. Still, they continued to follow me for the next fifteen blocks.

When I was thirteen, my abusive stepdad beat me unconscious. My mom called the police, and when they arrived, my stepdad convinced the officers that he had hit me in self-defense. They reasoned that it would probably be best if I "slept somewhere else" for the night to give myself some time to cool off. With no place else to go, I slept in the car.

I could go on with stories about racism that my friends and colleagues have shared with me, or I could just shrug, shake my head, and say, "George Floyd."

Some insist that when it comes to police racism, it's just a few bad apples, but that's not true. It's more than a few. This isn't political. It's a fact. Compared to the rest of the population, Black people are brutalized and murdered by the police at astronomically disproportionate rates. The way police departments across the United States select and train candidates to administer the critically important functions of law enforcement is deeply flawed. Because of the fundamental issues with the process, the pervasive ideology ingrained in police officers is deeply flawed as well.

By one estimate, Black men are two-point-five times more likely than white men to be killed by police during their lifetime. Over the life course, about one in every 1000 Black men can expect to be killed by police. Risk of being killed by police peaks between the ages of twenty and thirty-five for men and women and for all racial and ethnic groups.[20] And in another study, Black people who were fatally shot by police were twice as likely as white people to be unarmed.[21]

---

20   Frank Edwards et al. "Risk of being killed by police use of force in the United States by age, race–ethnicity, and sex," *Proceedings of the National Academy of Sciences of the United States of America,* (2019), doi: 10.1073/pnas.1821204116.

21   Justin Nix et al. "A Bird's Eye View of Civilians Killed by Police in 2015: Further Evidence of Implicit Bias," *Criminology and Public Policy* 16, no. 1 (2017):309-340, doi: 10.1111/1745-9133.12269.

American police officers feel justified in using violence when they feel "threatened," but they have been trained and conditioned to feel threatened, trained and conditioned to believe that they are in indefinite danger, and trained and conditioned to assume that each and every Black person is a threat to their own existence and a threat to the citizens of their country. As a result, police officers feel compelled to conquer Black people. Police officers pity themselves as misunderstood, undervalued, and unappreciated heroes. Blue heroes who are just doing their job. Blue heroes who are under constant physical attack by Black people. Blue heroes who are under constant political attack by liberals. Blue heroes whose lives matter more than the lives of those they take.

Their response to #BlackLivesMatter, the hashtag that became a movement after the murder-by-cop of George Floyd, is, of course, #BlueLivesMatter. This pro-police slogan, registered as a nonprofit in some states, presents itself as a cry for protection of police officers. Most important, it is the mantra for those who believe crimes against police should be treated as hate crimes.

Here's how the FBI identifies hate crimes:

Hate crimes are the highest priority of the FBI's civil rights program because of the devastating impact they have on families and communities. The Bureau investigates hundreds of these cases every year, and they work to detect and prevent incidents through law enforcement training, public outreach, and partnerships with community groups.

Traditionally, FBI investigations of hate crimes were limited to crimes in which the perpetrators acted based on a bias against the victim's race, color, religion, or national origin. In addition, investigations were restricted to those wherein the victim was engaged in a federally protected activity. With the passage of the Matthew Shepard and James Byrd, Jr., Hate Crimes Prevention Act of 2009, the Bureau also became authorized to investigate crimes committed against those based on biases of actual or perceived sexual orientation, gender identity, or disability.[22]

Police officer is a job title, the same as pilot, firefighter, teacher, or emergency medical technician. It is not your identity. When you take off your uniform, you look like everyone else. Contrary to what the Blue Lives Matter movement would have us believe, working in law enforcement is not the equivalent of being Black.

In writing for *HuffPost*, University of Southern California Center for Religion and Civic Culture contributor Jonathan Russell says that the movement attempts to

---

22 "What We Investigate: Hate Crimes." FBI. Accessed September 18, 2022. https://www.fbi.gov/investigate/civil-rights/hate-crimes.

make the profession of law enforcement equivalent to race. Further, he points out "the blue wall of silence," the belief that officers should protect other officers, including those in the wrong, because of their shared identity. While Black people are objects of hate crimes because of their skin color, police officers are members of a loyalty club. Blue lives have always mattered. The person in uniform will likely receive free meals, and the car ahead in line will pay for their coffee in the drive-through.

Russell calls the Blue Lives Matter hashtag "misrepresentative" and "disrespectful" and says, "This hashtag is wrong in so much as it connotes that the lives of law enforcement officers have failed to matter sufficiently in the broader public consciousness. It connotes that there is some culturally collective making up for that failure that needs to be done by parasitically drawing upon the form and cultural import of the black lives matter hashtag. In so much as it locates police life in a situation analogous to black life, it is wrongheaded, harmful, and offensive."[23]

Based on a review of more than two million 911 calls in two major U.S. cities, research concluded that white officers dispatched to Black neighborhoods fired their

---

23 Johnathan Russell. "Here's What's Wrong with #BlueLivesMatter," *HuffPost*, July 10, 2017, https://www.huffpost.com/entry/heres-whats-wrong-with-bl_b_10906348.

guns five times as often as Black officers dispatched for similar calls to the same neighborhoods.[24]

We don't even have to be engaged in a suspicious activity to be stopped or detained by police. In their eyes, being Black is a suspicious activity. In California, Black drivers were stopped at more than twice their share of the population in 2018 according to state data. Furthermore, they were searched and arrested more often.

Many times, Black drivers—or even drivers who are not Black but are driving a Black passenger—are pulled over for no reason. Oliver Baines, a former Central California councilmember who is Black and who was once a police officer, told *The Fresno Bee* that he was pulled over for speeding when he was a council member. When he denied the speeding charge, the officer who had stopped him said they were actually looking for a stolen vehicle, and his license plate was similar.

"Most of the times I've been stopped was for no reason," Baines said. "And I can tell you that any Black person will have a story identical to that."[25]

So, do blue heroes really exist? Blue heroes who are not predominantly racist? Blue heroes who do not vio-

24 Hoekstra, Mark and Carly Will Sloan. "Does Race Matter for Police Use of Force: Evidence from 911 Calls," *National Bureau of Economic Research,* (2020).

25 Manuela Tobias. "Data: Black drivers in Fresno stopped and searched more," *The Fresno Bee,* February 28, 2021.

lently suppress peaceful protests? Blue heroes who do not terrorize Black communities? Perhaps the concept of a "blue hero" only encompasses a few good apples propped up on a pedestal and purporting to represent the entire profession; perhaps the term "blue monster" would be more appropriate for the majority of police.

The Black community is at war; we are at war with a gang of straight white males with a substantial presence and pervasive influence in all fifty states. Straight white males with badges and guns who dominate our streets and who enforce their will upon us, without any limitation or accountability. The "guiding light" of law enforcement is not codified in any common law or state statute. Police officers are self-governed by longstanding police culture. Commanded to obey the unwritten rules of the blue brotherhood, commanded to participate in wrongful police conduct, commanded to actively ignore police administered injustice, commanded to look the other way when innocent Black citizens are killed, commanded to protect themselves first and foremost, commanded to honor the interests of the blue brotherhood above all else.

Officers who are fired for misconduct or who resign to avoid an investigation into such misconduct are routinely hired by another agency or department shortly thereafter. Timothy Loehmann, the Cleveland police officer who fatally shot twelve-year-old Tamir Rice in 2014, had previously resigned from another police department after being deemed unfit to serve. Did anyone review his file? What percentage of the U.S. police force has previously been fired or forced to resign for disciplinary reasons?

The blue brotherhood is shielded from being investigated for misconduct by state law and federal law, concepts of qualified immunity. Its members are commonly insulated from appropriate accountability by expansive union contracts. Derek Chauvin, the Minneapolis police officer who murdered George Floyd in 2020, had previously received over a dozen complaints against him for police misconduct. Did anyone monitor his performance? What percentage of the U.S. police force has received eighteen or more complaints against them?

WHAT HAS TO HAPPEN

Here's what has to happen. We have to police the police.

Civil rights attorney Alexis J. Hoag is the inaugural practitioner in residence at the Eric H. Holder, Jr., Initiative for Civil and Political Rights at Columbia University, working with both undergraduates and law school students at Columbia to introduce them to civil rights field work. In an interview with *Scientific American*, she said that data is currency. "We can create a national database of officer misconduct," she says. "The data collection that happens within police departments enabled experts in the stop-and-frisk litigation [against] the [New York City Police Department] to shine a spotlight on gross disparities: the rate of stops and searches of black and brown men and boys [coupled with] the low rate of actually acquiring contraband. They found that the rate of securing contraband from white individuals who had been stopped and frisked was so much higher because the police were actually using discretion. There's powerful data collection that happens in our criminal courts. There have been studies showing that, all factors being equal, judges are rendering longer and harsher sentences for black defendants. These judges are setting higher bail. You can isolate all these other factors, but race is the difference. That's very powerful— to be able to document and publish those findings.[26]

In one study, a requirement that officers file a report when they point their guns at people but do not fire was associated with significantly reduced rates of gun death.[27] From body cameras to defunding, ideas for

---

26   Lydia Denworth. "A Civil Rights Expert Explains the Social Science of Police Racism," *Scientific American*, June 4, 2020, https://www.scientificamerican.com/article/a-civil-rights-expert-explains-the-social-science-of-police-racism/.

27   Jennings, Jay and Meghan Rubado. "Preventing the Use of Deadly Force: The Relationship between Police Agency Policies and Rates of Officer-Involved Gun Deaths," *Public Administration Review*, no. 77 (2017): 217–226, doi: 10.1111/puar.12738.

policing the police prevail. In the meantime, our people are suffering arrest, humiliation, torture, and death. Our enemy isn't the police; it's racism, and it doesn't stop when someone puts on a uniform and swears to uphold the law.

WHAT WE CAN DO TO SAVE OUR OWN LIVES

How we deal with the police can mean the difference between life and death. Here's what has worked for me.

With each and every interaction I have with white people, especially white police officers, I am very aware of their perceptions. I try to put myself in their shoes. I try to imagine growing up in a white neighborhood with very little interaction with Black people. I try to think about what it would be like having your perception of Black people—me—based on what you see on Fox News, what you hear in rap music, and what you read in conservative media. Further, I think about the experiences the officer has had in the course of their job with people who look like me and that those interactions are more than likely the officer's only interactions with the Black community.

Another thing to recognize is that they're probably afraid of you. Whether their fear is warranted or not is irrelevant. Whatever the circumstances, any interaction between a white police officer and a Black person is initially clouded by the reality that the police officer is, at least at first, afraid. Fear exists on a spectrum. If the police officer gets too far right on the spectrum of fear, they will kill you. Speaking of fear, *that* is scary. With every encounter, your life's on the line. In some ways, this is true for both police officers *and* any Black people with whom they interact. It shouldn't be my responsibility to talk this officer (who has a gun) down from their irrational fear. However, their fear is something that I might be able to influence, and if I am able to do so, it could be the difference between life and death. If I can manage to deescalate the situation, it could save my life.

When you are approached or stopped by the police, admittedly, very little is within your control. Because of this reality, I have worked to identify the variables that *are* within my control. There are not many, but some of them might include the following: my behavior, my temperament, and my actions. When officers approach me, I greet them with a warm smile and a friendly hello. I make an extra effort to make sure they understand that I am not their enemy, that I mean them no harm, and that I'm not a criminal. I disarm them with small talk and pleasant conversation. While I may not be sure why the officer stopped me, we spend most of our interaction talking about the New England Patriots game on

Sunday or even the weather. I stay away from politics for obvious reasons.

WHEN YOU GET STOPPED— AND IT'S *WHEN*, NOT *IF*

Take a deep breath. Hold it in for a while. Then let that breath out. Calm down. When people get pulled over, they're upset, which is understandable. But the first thing you need to do is swallow that frustration and find an inner peace, however you do that—perhaps by thinking of a beloved parent, your spouse, your kids, or other people you love.

Remember the big picture. You're being pulled over by someone who is more than likely racist—and is more than likely afraid of you. That's a bad combination. If you are able to execute the strategy I'm about to prescribe, you must have a cool head. Cool heads prevail, and so will you.

As the officer approaches you, put your smile on early. I don't care if it's a real smile. Fake smiles work just as well. And keep breathing.

Let them say the first words, and respond with a friendly enthusiasm, as if this person is a school buddy or a friend from work. Be congenial and respectful, but do not be afraid. Be calm.

Be sure to sneak in, at some point in the conversation, some fact or detail about yourself.

"I'm driving home from coaching Little League."

"I'm on my way to teach math at the local elementary school."

"I'm meeting up with my girlfriend to watch *Seinfeld*."

"I'm picking up my daughter from preschool. She's four."

Humanize yourself, and help the officer see you for who you are. Be casual and relaxed. It will help the officer feel casual and relaxed too. If you can achieve that, you will live. If you cannot achieve that, you could be in danger.

Don't be in a hurry to end the interaction. Most people make the mistake of appearing agitated, annoyed, and flustered. They appear eager to get away from the officer. The truth, of course, is that we *are* eager to get away. Not because we are criminals but because police officers have a less than stellar reputation—they're scary—and we definitely have better things to do than to talk to them. But having said all of that, give the officer all the time they need. Criminals are in a hurry. You are not. You can do this all day.

Me: "How's your night going, officer?"

Me: "What's the craziest thing that's happened to you all day?"

They'll go on and on and on.

They've probably had a bad day and dealt with some really horrible people. You might be the one hundredth person they spoke to that day, and whatever number you are, make it clear that you're going to be one of the few who won't give them a hard time. Usually, unless you are suspected of a very serious crime, this methodology will work like a charm. If the interaction becomes more serious (we will cover Plan B later), the analysis changes slightly. But the approach should always be Plan A. This is for routine police interactions (which are most common and most likely to be the kind you will experience).

Police officers generally want only one thing from you: compliance. If you can give them that, they'll usually leave you alone.

Only they have the power to end the interaction.

Some might suggest that you ask, "Am I free to go?" but most of the time, if you've done everything I've suggested, it's not necessary. They'll tell you to have a nice day and be on your way. For plan A, at least, that's all you need to do.

It's important to remember that regardless of the injustices that led to your being stopped, mistreated, or misjudged, you are not going to win the fight that day. You must have the awareness to recognize that the police officer is in total control for the duration of that interaction. Once you are able to successfully exit and return safely home, you may finally and carefully review your options. Perhaps, because of the way you were treated, you feel it would be appropriate to file a formal complaint. Perhaps you recorded (secretly) damning video and/or audio evidence that you wish to share with the media. Or perhaps you may decide to move on with your life. You have these options after the fact, but certainly not during.

Know your rights

Plan A applies in all circumstances and at all times with the following important caveat: if you are being accused of doing something illegal outside of something minor, like speeding, you need to adapt to Plan B. If it becomes clear that the police officer has no intention of letting you go on your way or is asking you specific questions that suggest a belief that you committed a serious offense, do not answer any particular questions about the activity at issue. Be friendly and respectful, but decline to answer their questions. Instead, simply ask to speak with a lawyer. Even if you don't yet have an attorney, the police must provide you with an opportunity to contact a lawyer. Having a lawyer present is a fundamental right.

You always have the right to remain silent. If the police come to your home, you should not answer their questions or speak to them. Even if the officers have a warrant, stand silently and observe what they do, where they go, and what they take. Never consent to a search.

You can check the ACLU website for all of the basic rights you have, regardless of the circumstances. But here are some of the most important ones.

If you're detained, you must provide your name, address, and date of birth. However, that's all you're required to provide. A police officer must provide you with their I.D., name, agency, and badge number.

You may be patted down and any possessions within your reach may be searched if police reasonably suspect you pose an imminent threat of serious physical injury.

Write down everything you can remember about the police interaction, including officers' names and badge numbers.

Here's something you may not have thought about before: don't let the police fool you. They're legally allowed to lie to you to find out the information they're after. They'll also try to feed you the lie of all lies: "We'll go easier on you if you cooperate with us." There's no rule, no law that says they have to follow through on that, and many times, they do not. And then there's the famous, "Your friend X told us that you did Y." This is almost never true, and it is used as a tactic to get you to tell lies about your friend in retaliation. Then, they will use that lie as evidence against *both* of you.

What's your encounter?

Are you just talking, or are you being detained? Remember that there are three kinds of initial police encounters. These start with initial conversation. That might lead to the second encounter, the detention. From there, you have the worst encounter, the arrest. Here's how they play out.

The Conversation

I've said this earlier, but I need to emphasize it again: you are under no obligation to speak with law enforcement, and that includes an investigator, detective, police officer, FBI, ICE, or TSA. Be polite, but refuse to speak.

The Detention

A police officer may only detain you if they have a reasonable suspicion that you are involved in a crime.

"Reasonable suspicion" must be more than a mere hunch.

Police must be able to put their "reasonable suspicion" into words. Under the law, this is called the "articulable suspicion" provision.

You should ask, "Am I being detained? Am I free to leave? If not, why?"

The Arrest

The police may arrest you if they witness you breaking the law, have probable cause to believe you have committed a crime, or have an arrest warrant, signed by a judge, for your arrest.

If you commit an act of nonviolent civil disobedience, then you have broken the law.

Where can they search?

When making an arrest, the police are allowed to search you "to the skin." That means everywhere, including your vehicle and everything in it. The person searching must be the same sex that you are. Transdermal piercings may be removed.

The Miranda Rights

It is important to understand that you have a right to remain silent and to refuse to answer questions, but if you do choose to speak, anything you do say can and will be used against you. You also have the right to an attorney and to have them present while you're being questioned. If you cannot afford an attorney, they are required to appoint one to you for free.

WHAT ABOUT THE KIDS?

Part of the job of Black parents is teaching our kids how to act around the police. We must do that because our kids' lives are on the line.

Police officers present a serious threat to Black livelihood; police officers are dangerous to the perpetuation of our very existence. And although such a burden should never be imposed on a Black person, we must recognize this fact and learn to behave in a manner that offers us our best chance at surviving an encounter with a police officer.

At an early age, a Black child needs to know that interactions with police officers don't always go smoothly and that they can be dangerous. Books can be helpful. *Something Happened in Our Town: A Child's Story About Racial Injustice*, by Marianne Celano, Marietta Collins, Anne Hazzard, and Jennifer Zivoin, published by the American Psychological Association, follows a Black family and a white family as they discuss a police shooting of a Black man in their community.

Teens need to know what to do if they're stopped while driving. They need to politely ask for their parents, and they should not ask whether they are under arrest.

NPR interviewed a Black Chicago police officer about what parents need to teach their children and about what he has taught his own. Regardless of whether the young person is in the right or in the wrong, they must simply remain calm and do as they are asked, he advised.

He suggested these steps:

Turn off the ignition.

Roll down all of your windows—even if it's winter.

Explain where your license, registration, and insurance are before reaching for them.

"What I tell my kids, and the children I teach, is just comply," he said. "If the police officer asks you to do something, roll down the window and give them whatever they ask. And if it's an unlawful order, there are systems set in place where that police officer will be held accountable for [their] actions."

This guidance is a necessity to Black survival and an essential part of parenting Black children. Every Black family must have frequent, impassioned discussions aimed at ensuring their survival—painful discussions aimed at arming our children with skills with which to navigate and survive inevitable encounters with police officers. In defense of the Black children we love so deeply, we must communicate a stern but compassionate message:

> My child. I love you dearly, and I could never bear to lose you. We are Black, and we are beautiful, but we are at an extraordinary risk. Heed my words, my child.

My child. I love you dearly, and I could never bear to lose you. Police officers play an important role in our society, and their job is to protect and serve our community. But sometimes interactions do not go as they should. Sometimes police officers hurt us, and sometimes police officers kill us. Heed my words, my child.

My child. I love you dearly, and I could never bear to lose you. Avoid walking around with a hood up if possible; if it is raining, bring an umbrella. Wear your pants on or above your waist, never low-ride. Heed my words, my child.

My child. I love you dearly, and I could never bear to lose you. If you are pulled over while driving, turn off the ignition, roll down all of your windows (even if it is cold outside), and place both of your hands outside the window. If the officer gives you permission to move your hands back inside the car, place them directly on the steering wheel. Heed my words, my child.

My child. I love you dearly, and I could never bear to lose you. Ask for permission before reaching for your license, registration, or insurance. Once the officer acknowledges your question, explain where the item is located, announce what you are doing again, and then slowly retrieve it. Heed my words, my child.

My child. I love you dearly, and I could never bear to lose you. Always address the officer with respect. Use formal greetings such as sir, ma'am, or officer. Fake a smile and try to be friendly. Talk to them about sports or the weather. Ask them how their day is going. Try to act normal. Do not let them see how afraid you are. Your fear could make them feel threatened. Heed my words, my child.

My child. I love you dearly, and I could never bear to lose you. If a cop stops you on the street, remain calm. Check your words, body language, and emotions. Follow any and all instructions they give you. Make no sudden movements. If the reason is not offered, respectfully ask why you are being stopped. Heed my words, my child.

My child. I love you dearly, and I could never bear to lose you. If a situation with the police escalates for any reason, never resist. Never argue or raise your voice. Always comply with their commands. Never turn your back to them. Never walk away. Never run. If you are being arrested for no reason, let them arrest you. If you are being beaten, let them beat you. Your only goal is to get home to us safely. If your rights are violated, we have the right to file a formal complaint, but first, you must survive the interaction. Heed my words, my child.

My child. I love you dearly, and I could never bear to lose you. If you are questioned about any incident unrelated to a minor traffic violation, keep your mouth shut. Never make any statements until you are able to speak with a lawyer. Anything you say or do will be used against you. Heed my words, my child.

As painful as this conversation may be, it is necessary. And failing to faithfully follow these instructions could result in catastrophic consequences, deadly consequences.

CHAPTER 8

THE HEALTHCARE DECK & HOW IT'S STACKED AGAINST US

SUPPOSE YOU HAD A ONE in ten chance of dying younger than others in your age group. You would want to do something to change the odds. You would want those in healthcare to acknowledge and address that disparity. Yet approximately one in ten people in the United States can't change the odds because they don't have health insurance. And way, way too many of them look like us.

When you don't have health insurance, you may not have a primary care provider. Just as bad, you may not be able to afford the medications you need. In this chapter, I'm going to point out what you probably already suspect—that the healthcare system in America discriminates against Black people. It's a sad truth that I feel is necessary to explore because I believe it is something that we have the power to change if we approach it the right way. We have already proven we can change it—and we did so unexpectedly. More about that shortly.

Let's start with the basics, though: the social determinants of health. In other words, the things that determine your health starting with where you live and work. It's a matter of who gets to stay alive and thrive, and it comes down to the same way wealth, housing, and other aspects of life have long been determined: if you're Black, you go to the back. Why is it that, in this country, the maternal mortality for Black people is three to four times that of white Americans, even after accounting for poverty? Here's the answer: poor social determinants. Why are there fewer healthcare facilities in Black neighborhoods? Poor social determinants.

Why is there a difference between what "getting healthy" or "getting in shape" means to different people? While to some, it might mean joining a health club or giving up fast food. To others, it might mean simply making sure they have enough food to keep from going to bed hungry. Again, poor social determinants.

Perception can have a large impact on the quality of care you will receive. At age twenty, I was in a horrific car accident that nearly killed me and left me with a broken neck. I underwent numerous major surgeries, spent twenty-eight days in the hospital, and lost 40 percent of my body weight. I was in excruciating pain and needed constant heavy doses of morphine. But after being injected with opioids for weeks, the internal lining of my veins had become swollen, causing the veins to collapse and harden. The loss of circulation made my hands cold and caused sporadic, sharp pain in my arms. On my twenty-second day in the hospital, a couple of unfamiliar nurses entered my room in the middle of the night to test my blood.

Having great difficulty and quickly becoming frustrated, one muttered, "I can't find a single good vein. I don't know why we waste hospital beds on heroin addicts."

I was too weak to argue with her, but my mom wasn't. I thought she was asleep, but she quickly sprung up from her makeshift bed.

"Excuse me?" she said. "My son is not an addict!"

The perception of me, apparently, was that I looked like a drug addict. Do drug addicts receive the same quality of care as non-drug addicts? Do they get treated the same? No, they don't. Being a drug addict is a social detriment in the healthcare industry, the same as being Black; in some cases, these two conditions can even be conflated and confused for one another—like they were here. There is an assumption of wrongdoing and blame that overshadows the care Black people receive.

The World Health Organization defines social determinants of health as "the conditions in which people are born, grow, work, live, and age, and the wider set of forces and systems shaping the conditions of daily life."

According to the Center for Disease Control, social determinants of health are conditions in the places where people live, learn, work, and play that affect a wide range of health and quality-of-life risks and outcomes. Let's take a look at the most obvious.

- Economic stability and income
- Language and literacy skills
- Education access and quality
- Healthcare access and quality
- Neighborhood environment
- Transportation
- Job opportunities
- Air and water quality
- Access to nutritious foods
- Access to physical activity
- Racism
- Discrimination
- Violence

Social determinants of health, according to our own government, also contribute to wide health disparities and inequities. "For example, people who don't have access to grocery stores with healthy foods are less likely to have good nutrition. That raises their risk of health conditions like heart disease, diabetes, and obesity—and even lowers life expectancy relative to people who do have access to healthy foods."[28]

Henrietta Lacks was a Black woman who died of cervical cancer in 1951. Without her or her family's knowledge or consent, her cancer cells were biopsied and used to create the HeLa cell line. The HeLa cell line consists of the first human cells to be successfully grown in a lab and possesses a remarkably durable cell culture. More than one hundred corporations and pharmaceutical companies have realized enormous profits and achieved massive breakthroughs—including the advent of the polio vaccine, gene mapping, and in vitro fertilization—because of Ms. Lacks' involuntary biological contribution and the creation of the HeLa cell line. Almost all medicines that have been developed and marketed today have been tested on these cells. This is an outrageous example of racism in medicine, but unfortunately, this is only one instance out of many

---

28 "Social Determinants of Health." U.S. Department of Health and Human Services. Accessed September 18, 2022. https://health.gov/healthypeople/objectives-and-data/social-determinants-health.

which reflect the exploitation and inhumane treatment of Black people by medical professionals.

The Tuskegee Study represents yet another unethical experiment conducted on the cells of Black Americans. From 1932 to 1972 the U.S. Public Health Service performed an experiment on Black men in Macon County, Alabama, to determine the effects of latent syphilis if left untreated. The men were not told that they were participating in the study, nor were they made aware of the fact that they had contracted syphilis. In addition, despite the cure for syphilis being well known by the 1950s, they were never made aware of the cure either. Instead, they were repeatedly lied to by their doctors in the spirit of involuntary scientific research. Sound familiar? So, instead of being informed of their true illness and being prescribed penicillin, the treatment which would have saved their lives, the men were told they were being treated for "bad blood" and were given random placebos and other ointments known to be ineffective. Yes, the physicians just let them all die untreated. More than one hundred Black men who participated in this study were killed.

These physicians did not value Black lives. Instead, they believed that Black men were lustful, immoral, and barbaric—making them especially prone to venereal diseases—and therefore useful test subjects. According to Allen Brandt, the author of *Racism and Research*, at the time of this study, physicians studying the effects of emancipation on Black health generally held the belief that Black freedom had "caused the mental, moral, and physical deterioration of the [Black] population." Yes, they blamed their syphilis on their freedom.

The infamous Tuskegee Study is just one of all too many instances where the black population faces persecution in the form of medical racism. Like other aspects of systemic racism, this phenomenon is deep-rooted within the medical community. It demonstrates how misinformation surrounding racial superiority or inferiority is even apparent within seemingly scientific fields where the prejudice supersedes the actual biology.

Another project worth looking at is research by Kelly M. Hoffman, Sophie Trawalter, Jordan R. Axt, and M. Norman Oliver regarding racial bias in pain assessment and treatment recommendations and the false beliefs about biological differences between Blacks and whites among the medical community. This study was conducted on medical students and even practicing physicians wherein the participants were asked various medical questions about inaccurate stereotypes of Black people. The results were horrifying yet unsurprising.

A significant number of medical students believe Black people age more slowly and have super-

powered blood: 21 percent of first-year medical students had the incorrect assumption that Black people age slower than whites, and 29 percent thought that the blood of Blacks coagulated faster than whites. The latter, in particular, could obviously have catastrophic consequences in cases where a doctor wrongly assumes bleeding from a Black person is less of a concern. The assumption that black people's skin is thicker than that of white's, a disturbingly high 58 percent of first-year med students. This percentage only went down to 25 percent when looking at the bias of actual practicing residents.[29]

Other assumptions that harm Black people are the differences that are apparent between Black and white biology, and this most commonly arises when biased white people in the field fail to recognize the disadvantages that are present in the Black community or overestimate Black bodies while underestimating Black minds. This stems, of course, from the assumption that Black people are dumb and animalistic, only warranting credit for their physical and athletic prowess.

---

29   Kelly M. Hoffman et al. "Racial bias in pain assessment and treatment recommendations, and false beliefs about biological differences between blacks and whites," *Proceedings of the National Academy of Sciences of the United States of America*, (2016), doi: 10.1073/pnas.1516047113.

A significant number of medical students and physicians believe Black people feel less pain than whites: the study also examined the likelihood of Black patients to receive pain medication relative to their white counterparts. Even in instances where they are given the medication they need, the dose prescribed is lower. In another study by Knox H. Todd, referenced by Kelly M. Hoffman, Sophie Trawalter, Jordan R. Axt, and M. Norman Oliver, it was discovered that Black patients suffering from fractures received fewer analgesics than white patients (57 percent and 74 percent respectively). A significant difference, considering that the self-reported pain experienced by all patients was practically the same. This undoubtedly results in physicians erroneously withholding pain management medication to Black patients, causing Black patients to be forced to suffer greater amounts of pain than their white counterparts.

When looking at children with appendicitis in a study of almost one million patients, it was seen that Black children were less likely to receive medication to relieve pain, specifically the appropriate type expected when treating severe pain: opioids. A different study explored the differences in pain management among patients with metastasizing cancer. The takeaway was that merely 35 percent of patients categorized as a racial minority received the correct treatment as officially recognized by the World Health Organization, compared to 50 percent of white patients.[30] These results show that there still remains a significant problem of false racial assumptions and racial bias among medical students.

There are also other issues that arise in the medical community surrounding the lack of consideration and understanding of darker skin and how skin complexion could influence the conclusions of standard medical procedures, examinations, or tests. Dangerous problems for Black patients can arise when white skin is the default.

For example, oximeters, which measure the oxygen saturation in your red blood cells, have been used in at-home tests to evaluate the condition of COVID-19. This is because low oxygen levels can arise suddenly in people who test positive for the virus and are often an indicator of the most severe cases. A study performed at the University of Michigan measured the blood oxygen level of 1,333 white patients and 276 Black patients using a pulse oximeter and then compared it to the arterial blood gas test. This study found that the test overestimates arterial oxyhemoglobin saturation in individuals with dark skin at a rate of nearly four times greater

30   Charles S. Cleeland et al. "Pain and treatment of pain in minority patients with cancer," *Annals of Internal Medicine* 127, no. 9 (1997), doi: 10.7326/0003-4819-127-9-199711010-00006.

than white patients.[31] Specifically, pulse oximetry over-estimated oxygen levels 3.6 percent of the time in white patients, but got it wrong nearly 12 percent of the time in Black patients.[32]

Pulse oximetry uses light, which absorbs differently through darker pigmented skin. Overlooking the way things may differ for different skin complexions also becomes problematic in medical school where students are not taught the ways a skin condition, for example, may appear differently on darker skin, and then, of course, there are conditions that show up predominantly on black skin that are also not taught.

So here's the question. How many times has a false oximeter reading cost a dark-skinned patient their life? If the physician checks the oxygen level of a Black patient hospitalized with COVID-19 using a pulse oximeter and fails to recognize their low blood oxygen level—the physician would have no way of confirming whether other emergent steps are required to improve the patients breathing and blood oxygenation. The consequence of this may be death.

---

31 Tara Parker-Pope. "Oximeters May Be Less Accurate for Black People. Should You Use One?" *New York Times*, December 23, 2020, https://www.nytimes.com/2020/12/23/well/live/pulse-oximeter-black.html.

32 Tara Parker-Pope. "Oximeters May Be Less Accurate for Black People. Should You Use One?" *New York Times*, December 23, 2020, https://www.nytimes.com/2020/12/23/well/live/pulse-oximeter-black.html.

Would our medical community tolerate the consequent of possible death if the same problem or inaccuracy occurred with respect to lighter-skinned patients? Do I even have to answer the question? No, probably not. I would not think so.

All people should be prioritized and properly treated and cared for by the medical community, yet it isn't happening. What can we do about it?

A medical student, Malone Mukwende, took note of this in 2019 and published a book outlining these key differences called *Mind the Gap: A Handbook of Clinical Signs in Black and Brown Skin*.[33] Mukewende wrote that since his first class at St George's medical school at the University of London, he noticed a lack of teaching about darker skin tones and how certain symptoms appear differently in those who aren't white. His book highlights the cause of many of the issues we have discussed in this chapter.

"Not only was there an absence of imagery to highlight the difference, but students were not instructed on the correct terminology to describe conditions that appear on darker skin," Mukwende said.

Peter Tamony, a doctor and educator, praised Mukwende's work as critical and said, "Our methods of teach-

---

33   Malone Mukewende. *Mind the Gap: A Handbook of Clinical Signs in Black and Brown Skin* (London: St George's University of London, 2019).

ing were unfairly disadvantaging and 'othering' students from black and minority ethnic groups," and asked, "Are we adequately training our students to be competent healthcare professionals who can detect important clinical signs in all patient groups?"

Sometimes asking the right question is as important as finding the answer. Recognizing that this is an issue is the first step. Training doctors and medical professionals to care about and understand the differences that exist between Black and white people, and the differences that do not, is essential to assuring competent medical practice. And this training begins in medical school.

All people should be able to access preventive care and treatment for chronic illnesses, yet often people don't get recommended healthcare services, such as cancer screenings, because they don't have a primary care provider. Other times, it's because they live too far away from healthcare providers who offer them. Interventions to increase access to healthcare professionals and improve communication—in person or remotely—can help more people get the care they need.

I DO NOT ACCEPT...

I do not accept that Black Americans have a higher prevalence of chronic disease and do worse if they have a chronic disease.

I do not accept that Black Americans receive less preventive care and fewer screenings for cancer and heart disease.

I do not accept that Black Americans get less testing for heart disease when they show up to an emergency room.

I do not accept that access to quality care, rather than genetics, contributes to a two-point-five times higher prostate cancer mortality rate for Black men compared to non-Hispanic white men.

I do not accept that Black Americans have worse outcomes when they get treated for cancer.

I do not accept that Black Americans have a lifespan that is years shorter than that of white Americans—in some cities, a difference in life expectancy of ten to twenty years!

I do not accept that Black mothers and infants die at two to four times the rate that white mothers and infants do.

I do not accept it. We cannot accept it.

To accept it is to accept the racism that is entrenched in our healthcare system and in our larger social system in this country.

WHEN YOUR ZIP CODE IS A DEATH SENTENCE

Although the hospital system is supposed to serve people in the community, it does not have public health accountability. As a result, disparities of care exist in nearly adjacent zip codes, disparities that can mean a fifteen- to twenty-year difference in lifespan. Just think. Moving over a few miles and living in a different zip code could mean the difference between living to the age of sixty-five versus the age of eighty-five. That's true in all the cities in our country. It's true in Chicago. If you're in the Loop (one of Chicago's seventy-seven designated community areas, consisting of the central business district of the city and the main section of downtown) or out of the Loop, your life expectancy can vary. DePaul researchers found life expectancy in Englewood to be among the lowest in the city at sixty-seven to seventy-two years, while life expectancy in the Loop and Near North was eighty-one to eighty-four years.

The contaminated water crisis of Flint, Michigan, was a tragic example of a lack of a good public health system in place. Between 6,000 and 12,000 children were exposed to drinking water with high levels of lead. Furthermore, the Flint water supply change was considered a possible cause of an outbreak of Legionnaires' disease that killed twelve people and affected another eighty-seven in the county.

Lack of a good public health system in place is also the reason the United States was caught completely off guard and incapable of managing the COVID crisis. We didn't have a surveillance system in place. We didn't have the infrastructure and protocols for a pandemic preparedness program.

Those are some of the fallouts we're seeing as a result of not having a strong public health system in place and depending solely on one system of access to care. Unfortunately, many of you already know that public health systems are an important part of the solution, as many Black people rely on them, which is particularly problematic considering how underfunded they are.

PUBLIC HEALTH ISSUES OVER THE DECADES

▸ 1890s: Water pollution, milk sanitation, hygiene education, bacteriology, infectious diseases

▸ 1900–1910s: Infectious diseases, municipal health, water, standardization of health data

▶ 1920s: Local health departments, water, milk, training standards, personal hygiene, infectious disease, close-quartered living

▶ 1930s: Communicable diseases, sanitation, laboratories, statistics, food safety, housing, education, poverty, medical care, war

▶ 1940s: Professional standards, evaluations of schools of public health, infectious diseases, functions of local health departments

▶ 1950s: Push for federal agency solely focused on health and federal health funds for states, health legislation and advocacy, accreditation of public health schools, polio, pasteurization, and food safety

▶ 1960s: Equality within public health workforce, integration, the War on Poverty, birth control, public health training, environmental issues, consumer protection, human rights

▶ 1970s: War, global health, drug abuse, new technology, upgraded health facilities

▶ 1980s: AIDS, teen pregnancy, nuclear safety

▶ 1990s: Clinton Health Reform Plan, Gulf War impacts, tobacco, managed healthcare, vaccinations, E. coli, AIDS, school safety

- ▸ 2000s: Emergency preparedness, obesity, climate change, built environment

- ▸ 2010s: President Barack Obama's Affordable Care Act, food safety, child nutrition, EPA regulations

If you look at the history of public health, you can see how the system changed over the decades. Here's what I don't have to tell you—something you already know because you've seen it or you know someone who has. *The defunding of our public health system does not affect all communities and all people the same.* It's as simple as that and as tragic. Poor people, those who live in inner cities and those who live in rural environments, suffer the most. We're going to have to have a vigorous public health system in place to complement the medical system, which we did have in the past, before the defunding and before the emphasis on individual patient responsibility.[34]

So, what does a strong public healthcare system look like? I'm not a medical professional, but I've spoken with some of them, and almost all agree that first of all, you would actually have a lot more professionals trained in public health and working in a public health service. Look at public health offices in towns. They're relatively small, if they exist at all, with meager staffing.

---

34 "Our History," American Public Health Association. Accessed September 18, 2022. https://www.apha.org/about-apha/our-history.

Let's take a look at how a major California public health department defines itself. According to its website, the core functions of Los Angeles County Department of Public Health include: Assessment, Policy Development, and Assurance.

The ten essential public health services published by the Centers for Disease Control and Prevention are listed below and categorized under the appropriate core function.

I. Assessment:

1. Monitor health status to identify and solve community health problems (e.g. community health profile, vital statistics, and health status)

2. Diagnose and investigate health problems and health hazards in the community (e.g. epidemiologic surveillance systems, laboratory support)

II. Policy Development:

3. Inform, educate, and empower people about health issues (e.g. health promotion and social marketing)

4. Mobilize community partnerships and action to identify and solve health problems (e.g. convening and facilitating community groups to promote health)

5. Develop policies and plans that support individual and community health efforts (e.g. leadership development and health system planning)

III. Assurance:

6. Enforce laws and regulations that protect health and ensure safety (e.g. enforcement of sanitary codes to ensure safety of the environment)

7. Link people to needed personal health services and ensure the provision of healthcare when otherwise unavailable (services that increase access to healthcare)

8. Assure competent public and personal healthcare workforce (e.g. education and training for all public healthcare providers)

9. Evaluate effectiveness, accessibility, and quality of personal and population-based health services (e.g. continuous evaluation of public health programs)

10. Research for new insights and innovative solutions to health problems (e.g. links with academic institutions and capacity for epidemiologic and economic analyses)[35]

---

35 "Resources Organized by Essential Services." Centers for Disease Control and Prevention. July 18, 2022. https://www.cdc.gov/nceh/ehs/10-essential-services/resources.html.

All else being equal, we will not solve the dilemma we're in through the singular lens of the medical mind-set and the medical system we have in place. It doesn't have the tools. It doesn't have a conceptual frame. It doesn't have the approach to do this. And it doesn't have the authority. We need a complementary public health system.

When you don't have a public health system or a primary care system, what you're going to have is a high-cost system that is highly reactive and focused on end-stage disease. You can't ask hospitals to fix that problem. You can't ask doctors to fix that problem. You've got to put a public health system in place that fixes that problem.

MONEY TALKS

We have a system of payment in this country that was developed by the American Medical Association, which favors specialists over primary care and also favors procedures over prevention. The system is set up so that specialists get paid more than primary care.

Washington is manipulated and invented by constituents but also by lobbyists. Big pharma has an amazingly strong lobby. The insurance companies have a strong lobby. The American Medical Association and other medical associations and societies have strong lobbies. Public health does not, and it is not getting enough attention because public health traditionally treats those without the power to lobby for it.

THE GOOD NEWS

We need to get more people trained in public health. We must build public health systems back up to resource them, to staff them, and to give them the authority that they need to do the job they're supposed to do. On that topic, there is good news. As a result of the pandemic, there has been an increase in students' interest in going into public health. From fall of 2019 to fall of 2020, there was a 23 percent jump in applicants for masters and doctoral programs in public health schools, according to the Association of Schools and Programs of Public Health.[36]

And the American Public Health Association reports that in March 2021, the number of applicants using the ASPPH's Schools of Public Health Application Service was 40 percent higher than the year before, with more than 24,000 prospective students considering the field. As the association points out, it is a significant change

---

36 Andrew Joseph. "Driven by the Pandemic and the 'Fauci Effect,' Applicants Flood Public Health Schools." *Stat*, March 17, 2021, https://www.statnews.com/2021/03/17/driven-by-pandemic-applicants-flood-public-health-schools/.

for a field beset by funding cuts, early retirements, and people leaving to pursue other occupations.[37]

I mentioned earlier that I think this situation can change—and because of an unlikely reason, and that is COVID. The pandemic revealed what we always suspected. It shined a bright light on social injustice and inequity in general, racial injustice and inequity in particular. It brought both to the forefront of public health. According to the CDC, "It has highlighted that health equity is still not a reality as COVID-19 has unequally affected many racial and ethnic minority groups, putting them more at risk of getting sick and dying from COVID-19."[38]

The pandemic forced those in healthcare to move and change rapidly, despite what they had been told was not possible. It pointed out the system's shortcomings in a way no one could deny.

It exposed "glaring gaps in care for rural and low-income communities, as well as people of color. The lack of domestic manufacturing capacity for critical supplies like protective equipment forced nurses to reuse masks

---

37 Aaron Warnick. "Interest in Public Health Degrees Jumps in Wake of Pandemic: Applications Rise." *The Nation's Health*, August 2021. https://www.thenationshealth.org/content/51/6/1.2.

38 "What is Health Equity?" Centers for Disease Control and Prevention. July 1, 2022. https://www.cdc.gov/coronavirus/2019-ncov/community/health-equity/race-ethnicity.html.

and dress in garbage bags. Patient care unrelated to COVID-19 suffered."[39]

In addition to revealing race and gender bias, the pandemic has shown that we did not have a public health system in place to deal with health crises.

Yet, the pandemic forced healthcare to move rapidly to telemedicine. It revealed the need for mental health services. It showed that healthcare can and must change and that providers must think beyond the social determinants. It showed that we can move forward, and we can't go back.

An equitable healthcare system is a starting place. Of course, it won't magically solve discrimination and the socioeconomic discrepancies that contribute to poor health outcomes among our people. It's not the whole solution, but it is part of it.

---

39 Clason, Lauren and Mary Ellen McIntire. "How the pandemic changed healthcare, one year later." *Roll Call*, March 10, 2021. https://rollcall.com/2021/03/10/how-the-pandemic-changed-health-care-one-year-later/.

CHAPTER 9

THE CHALLENGE & THE TRIUMPH OF BLACK PARENTHOOD

A Black Monster

Yesterday, the Black dad came home. His eyes were tired but warm, his skin marked by deep lines, engraved there by hate. He put on a brave face for his family. Things were not okay.

Yesterday, the Black dad came home. He hung up his coat on the hook by the door. He slipped off his shoes and went straight upstairs. Things were not okay.

Yesterday, the Black dad came home. He was exhausted to the bone and defeated by the end of his second shift. He was not okay and could not muster the strength to pretend that he was. Things were not okay.

Yesterday, the Black dad came home. He burned with the rage the world had jammed down his throat. And he took it out on those around him, trying to release the pain that consumed him. Things were not okay.

Today, the Black dad did not come home. The hook on the wall sits naked without the comforting weight of his coat. His shoes are not lined up in the front closet. The house is empty of his tired, often flawed love. Things are not okay.

Today, the Black dad did not come home. His Black humanity was ripped from his body for going ten kilometers too fast. His face is on TV, and people are talking about him. His face is stripped of any warmth or humanity now—raw with bitterness, the face of a thug. Things are not okay.

Today, the Black dad did not come home. They repackaged him, slandered him, and regurgitated a new narrative, something

*everyone could swallow. A Black father, a
Black brother, a Black uncle, a Black friend.
But also a Black monster. The unfortunate
yet unavoidable death of a Black monster.
Nobody thinks twice about the murder of
a monster. Things are not okay.*

*Today, the Black dad is gone. He does not
breathe anymore. And now, neither can I.*

Promoting responsible parenting is more important
now than ever. The world is demanding positive change,
and Black parents need to be at the helm.

Though both Black motherhood and Black fatherhood are equally important and equally worthy of discussion, much of the focus of this chapter will be on
Black fatherhood. This is not because I feel that Black
motherhood is any less important of a subject. Such a
notion could not be further from the truth.

Part of the fundamental premise of this book and my
very own personal belief is that the only ones who can
be granted the authority to speak and publish regarding
topics and ideas unique to a particular gender, race, ethnicity, or other unalienable conditions are those with
firsthand experience with said condition.

I feel that my time here, for the purposes of this
book, is best dedicated to the discussion of my own

experiences and to the discussion of Black fatherhood. I am not a woman; I am a man. I am not a mother; I am a father. Therefore, I cannot speak from the perspective of women or mothers. I can say, though, that I truly appreciate all of the women and mothers in my life, especially the mothers of my children and my mother. The influence mothers have on young boys and girls is well documented and well celebrated, deservingly so.

I did not have a loving father. I will come right out and say it. My experiences with father figures as a child are painful to think about. I did not meet my biological father until I was about fifteen, and by that point, the damage had been done. I won't say it was too late, because it meant a lot to meet him. But I must acknowledge that it was extremely difficult growing up without my "real" dad around. My stepfather did not care about himself, and therefore, he could never care about me. He treated my entire family poorly, but I definitely got the worst of it. Stepchildren always do.

So, what's worse? Neglect or physical and psychological abuse? I don't know—both are pretty bad.

At age fourteen, I had just played really well in a basketball game. It was difficult for my mom to attend my games regularly, so I was excited to tell her how it went.

I bragged to her, "I had twenty-five points and ten rebounds!"

My mom was thrilled.

"Yay!" she said.

My stepfather, who had overheard our conversation, shouted from the other room, "Well, you're gonna end up in jail or on drugs anyway, so who cares?"

Needless to say, he was not my biggest fan. And unfortunately, he was one of the only Black men I knew.

At age thirteen, on a Sunday after church, I went to my best friend Sawyer's house to play video games. Sawyer's mom knew my curfew was 9:00 p.m. and thought it would be fine if we left by 8:50 p.m. She drove me home, and I arrived at 9:05 p.m., five minutes late. My stepdad grounded me for a week.

"I'm only five minutes late! And it wasn't my fault," I said.

"Go to your room now, or your punishment will increase."

I did not move.

"F-you. This is BS," I shouted in frustration.

"One, two, three...two weeks...one, two, three...three weeks...one, two, three...four weeks." By the time he was finished counting, I was grounded for three months. I was seething with anger. Before I walked upstairs, I tossed my baseball cap at him like a Frisbee. It bounced off his gut and fell harmlessly to the ground, but he supposedly felt "threatened," so he chased me to the stairwell and punched me square in the back of the head. Out cold. I woke up in the car being taken to stay with my cousins for a while.

From there, I bounced around—living at different friend's houses and on random couches for a few years until I could get on my feet. My story is not all that special. Many of you can probably relate, and many of you could probably share worse. Growing up to become a responsible, kind, independent, hardworking human being without a loving and present father figure is tough—and statistically unlikely. I got lucky.

The necessity of a fatherly influence in a traditional household to maintain familial stability is a narrative as old as time itself. The narrative goes like this: a paternal presence is integral to critical developmental aspects of children and adolescents, namely behavior, academics, health, and overall well-being. Fathers who are properly involved and invested in their children's lives dutifully take on beneficial parenting responsibilities, including academic intervention and clear constructive discipline.

Competent fatherhood should be a collective societal goal. With this in mind, consider the consequences that might arise when an individual or a family unit lacks such an invaluable influence—particularly, the implications of this deficit within a Black family. In what way is this intertwined with the Black condition and with the systematic racism that is still rampant today? How does Black parenthood specifically affect the development of today's Black youth and communities?

The go-to argument of conservatives and white folks typically reasons that Black fathers are mainly uninvolved if not purely absent from their family's lives. The dynamic of the conventional, traditional family is put up on a pedestal, even while the unfortunate reality that the make-up of a household is not controlled by the people most affected (namely the children of an absent father) is ignored. No abandoned child chooses a life of instability and persistent feelings of worthlessness. Any solution poised to remedy the issue of absent or unavailable Black fathers must take this factor into account, but being there for your children is not always easy or straightforward.

In law school, I was a summer intern for a Federal Judge. For two months, I sat and observed trials, conferences, sentencing hearings, and other courtroom activities, and I suppose I did a little bit of work too. There is a particular sentencing hearing that will be forever burned into my memory. A sentencing hearing is held after the trial and verdict has been rendered. The purpose of the hearing is for the judge to rule on the convict's sentence upon the consideration of the defendant's testimony, the prosecution's sentencing recommendations, and rule-based sentencing guidelines for the particular offense committed. This particular man had been convicted of possession of cocaine with the intent to distribute. For the sake of maintaining his anonymity, let's call him Lewis. He was a married forty-three-year-old Black man with three daughters. Lewis had just been convicted of his third drug-related offense. None of his prior offenses were particularly severe, and certainly did not involve violence. Lewis was but a small-time cocaine dealer living in Section 8 housing in Newark, New Jersey, but unbeknownst to him and his three children, Lewis was about to be sentenced to life in prison.

The prosecutors in the case filed what's known as an 851 notice. This filing is named after the section of the U.S. Code from which it was derived. The filing of this notice in this particular context evoked what's referred to as the "Three Strikes" law. This law ties the hands of judges, taking away any discretion they have over sentencing, and routinely sends harmless, non-violent drug offenders to prison for life. This all means that the judge, unfortunately, had no choice but to sentence Lewis to die behind bars for a minor drug charge. I will never forget observing his sentencing.

In this case, the judge had very little discretion to make a downward departure from the sentencing guidelines. Usually, the sentencing hearing provides a mean-ingful opportunity for the convicted individual to plead their case and explain to the judge why they are deserv-ing of favorable treatment and a lighter sentence. Lewis poured his heart out. He explained what fatherhood meant to him. He described how hard he tried to gain legitimate employment. He shared that he had applied to hundreds and hundreds of jobs, but nobody would hire him because of his prior felony conviction. He expressed his regret and sadness over feeling trapped. He passionately told the judge how much he loved his daughters. With tears streaming down his face, Lewis explained that he never wanted or intended to sell drugs again. His family was financially compromised, and they were on the verge of being evicted from their apartment. Unable to find a "real" job, Lewis expressed how he felt "forced" to sell drugs again in order to sur-vive—in order to support his family—in order to keep a roof over their head.

"This is all I know how to do, and this is all anyone will pay me to do," Lewis said defeatedly.

The judge responded with a tone of regret, saying softly, "Sorry. There is nothing I can do."

Lewis burst into a loud, full-blown cry, and then he passionately shouted, "My daughters need me, Judge. Please don't take their daddy away. Please."

This was gut wrenching to witness. I truly felt for this man. But over time, my empathy for and understanding of Lewis and others like him grew even greater, especially now that I have children of my own. Now that I know what loving your child feels like. Now that I know what promising to be there for them, no matter what, feels like.

But there are certain conditions I cannot relate to or understand. I do not know what it feels like to be raised on the streets, for all your friends and family to be drug dealers and gang affiliated. I do not know what it feels like to have the most important people in my life taken away from me.

Contrary to what many in our society may say or believe, Lewis is not a bad father. Lewis and his family are victims of circumstance. His condition and the consequences for his actions are created and promulgated by institutional racism. What does it mean to be a good father? What does it mean to be a good parent? Does it mean that you would do anything for your children? That you would sacrifice your life for them? Lewis checks those boxes. The tragedy of his story lies in his belief that he was trapped and incapable of doing anything productive outside of drug dealing. The narrative of "bad" fathers who spend their children's lives behind bars needs to be rethought. The blame and the responsibility needs to be re-shifted. This is not to say that Lewis lived his life perfectly. I am sure he has many regrets. I am sure that, if he could, he would do many things differently. But a "justice" system that takes a man's life away...that takes three little girls' daddy away, forever, for dealing a little cocaine is problem number one.

A CDC study found that about 2.5 million Black fathers were living with their children and about 1.7 million were officially living apart from them. Counting by the number of children, rather than the number of fathers, presents a different picture. The Census Bureau reports that slightly more than half of black children live in homes headed by one parent—which is usually, but not always, the mother. This is explained, in part, by "non-co-residential" fathers having more children. It's also true that Black children are more likely than others to be born out of wedlock. Millions of kids live with their fathers half the time, or at least part of the time, through joint custody arrangements. But children generally have one legal address, which is particularly important for purposes of determining school districts. Most often, the legal address is the mother's. This is a major reason that fatherlessness statistics in general are overblown. Fathers' homes all too often are not counted officially as being "homes with children." (Also, some unmarried couples live together, making the marriage statistics even more misleading.)[40]

Black fathers are statistically more likely to live away from their children than fathers belonging to other racial groups. Even so, Black fathers who live outside of their children's household are reportedly more involved in raising those children than fathers of other racial groups, and they also share parental responsibilities more effectively than other fathers residing outside of the familial home. However, Black fathers are faced with unique challenges that impede their ability to remain a consistent source of developmental and financial support for their families, an important factor that is often overlooked.

Economic pressures are a particular challenge, especially given the unfairly disproportionate rate of incarceration of Black men to men of other racial groups. These inequities in the criminal justice system fuel difficulties for Black fathers in their efforts to secure and maintain steady jobs, a fact that puts pressure on their marriages and their families. It is an unsurprising fact, then, that impoverished communities have higher rates of child abandonment. This ongoing struggle is a product of generations of economic disadvantage that Black

40 Josh Levs. "They're Dragging out the Absent Black Fathers Myth Again. Can we Give it a Rest?" *Newsweek*, June 5, 2020. https://www. newsweek.com/absent-black-fathers-myth-racism-1509085.

people have faced over generations. Black families are still in recovery from years and years of inequality of wealth and opportunity, something that is particularly difficult when racial inequality and racist attitudes are still prevalent today.

Like the "welfare queen" myth, the "bad dad" stereotype is based on the stereotyping of Black people as lazy and unfit parents—and like the welfare queen, it's a stereotype not grounded in fact: a 2013 CDC survey noted Black fathers actually tend to spend more time with their children than white fathers—whether they live with their children or not.[41]

And like the "welfare queen" myth, the "bad dad" stereotype is also rooted in state-sanctioned violence against Black people in the U.S.—often via the war on drugs and subsequent over-policing of Black communities.

Education is at the root of the historic economic inequality that Black men face. Black men encounter overwhelming obstacles in their quest to graduate from college and frequently finish with more debt than their white counterparts. These harsh realities undoubtedly affect the decision of Black youths to even attend college at all, especially if they are saddled with the respon-

41   Oliver C. Haug. "'Bad Dads' and the Policing of Black Parent-hood." *Ms. Magazine*, August 28, 2020, https://msmagazine.com/2020/08/28/abby-johnson-white-parents-bad-dads-and-the-policing-of-black-parenthood/.

sibility of supporting impoverished families and can-not simultaneously satisfy the astronomical cost of a post-secondary education.

Another obstacle faced by young Black men are those presented by mental and physical health chal-lenges. Black men have lower life expectancies than white men, often as a result of poverty and inability to practice healthy habits, which is also damaging to their mental health. These aspects of inequality feed off each other in a vicious cycle of financial, physical, and men-tal struggles.

The media and pop culture are major culprits in perpetuating negative stereotypes in connection with the ability of Black men to fulfill the duties of father-hood. Endless depictions of absent and unfaithful Black fathers appear in popular culture, tearing down and stigmatizing Black men and their families. Coupled with the obstacles young Black men already face, the prevalence of these negative, overblown stereotypes in the media young men consume inevitably sets them up for failure. These stigmatic narratives have taken root in the collective belief systems of society, fueling sys-temic racism and in some circumstances, reinforcing the hopeless cycle of Black fathers failing to meet the challenge of adequately supporting their families. Far too often, Black fathers are written off by society as a lost cause.

So why are any of these issues that affect young Black men relevant to addressing problems associated with Black fatherhood? Context is everything. Analyzing or criticizing any subject is fruitless without considering all related variables. Effectively solving a problem is impossible without understanding why it occurred in the first place. Otherwise, any solution is temporary or insignificant at best. Say you're a doctor; you can treat the symptoms of a patient who is having seizures, but to best manage the condition, it is imperative to get to the root of why that patient is seizing in the first place.

Building Black fathers up and encouraging dialogues about Black fatherhood are crucial factors in effecting change. Ending the stigmatization of Black fatherhood in popular culture and the media is one place to start. A more positive narrative, of the Black father who spends time with his children, nurturing them, helping them with their homework, teaching them critical life lessons, taking the time to play catch or hit a tennis ball around, should be substituted for the typical, recurring narrative of the absent Black father.

Fellas, how can we achieve this? It starts with us. It starts with our perception of fatherhood and what constitutes doing "enough" in that category. We must change the definition of what fatherhood means. We must begin to truly consider fathers and mothers equal. We must begin to expect nothing less from Dad than we do from Mom. The stereotypes surrounding parenting roles in our communities are unacceptable. Far too often, we apportion an unfair and unequal responsibility on Mother's shoulders in the area of child rearing. Not only does this contribute to gender inequality and harm the professional aspirations of Black women, but it is harming our children.

Children who lack the care and attention of both of their parents often suffer from mental illness, obesity, addiction, and even imprisonment. Father-deprived youth are hungry for role models and are ultimately more vulnerable to illegal activities. Our behavior in this manner is subtly teaching our children about the roles of men and women. Black parenthood matters, and Black men are responsible for no less than 50 percent of the job. Let's tolerate nothing less. It begins here and now. I challenge you to commit to doing your fair share. There are no excuses. Your job is not more important than the job your child's mother could be working during the same hours. Her opportunity to earn, achieve, and grow professionally is just as important as yours. It starts with me, and it starts with you. Let's dedicate ourselves to being the best fathers we can be. Let's be equal parents.

Despite incredible efforts made by single mothers, the absence of Black fathers in homes causes stress and depression on both parents' parts, which often damages the development of the affected children. Black children are frequently dismissed at a very young age, impeding their ability to thrive. We all need to examine our own personal biases and the stereotypes that cause so much damage among Black youth. As the number of conventional family units decreased in the early 1960s, poverty and crime rates increased, revealing the undeniable correlation between adequate parental role models and economic status. In a study conducted in 1965, sociologist Daniel Moynihan discovered that the main indicator of generational poverty was not necessarily race, but rather being born to unmarried parents—the underlying subtext being that most children born under these circumstances lack their father's involvement.

There is no joy in life greater than parenthood. From the moment I held my first-born girl in my arms, I knew I would never be the same. I saw the world differently after that. As much importance as I thought my life had before she arrived, it quadrupled that day. I will never forget how it felt. I remember staring deeply into her eyes and silently promising that I would always be there for her—that I would always protect her—that I would give her everything—that I would be the best dad in the world for her. Her tiny eyes stared right back at me with a calm ferocity, as if to say, "Damn, right. You better."

We cannot choose our parents, and we cannot choose our children. But when we bring a child into this world, whether intentionally or not, we have a responsibility. A big one. We have a duty to be the best we can be. We have a duty to provide that tiny little human being with the best possible life we can imagine. We owe them that. In exchange for the blessing of their unconditional love, we owe them the world. Fathers, pound your chest twice and say, "I will" if you're committed. Pound your chest twice and say, "I will" if you are committed to reporting for duty every day. Pound your chest twice and say, "I will" if you love your child or children and you're up to the job.

CHAPTER 10

BUILDING ONE COMMUNITY THROUGH BLACK RESILIENCE

THERE CAN BE NO LASTING progress in the area of race relations in America as long as the Black community continues to buy into the false narrative that white people are in control and therefore are responsible for "fixing" racism. Black success in America is not dependent on white people becoming more socially conscious or more apologetic or more "aware" of their privilege. These ideas are actually spread mostly by savior types flexing their white power and bragging of their influence. White people are no longer our masters. It is time for us to rise above our fears of white mistreatment. We must rise and know our worth. We must rise and know our power.

Racism hurts, but it cannot stop us. Just as our ancestors broke their steel shackles and freed themselves from bondage, it is time for us to free our minds from the false prison of white superiority. The current political landscape is dominated by blatantly racist talking heads and white saviors preaching about their wokeness. Propaganda regarding racism and the power white people have over our communities has dominated news coverage. These conversations are being seen and heard by our Black children, our youngest and most impressionable, the future of Black America. These ideas are untrue and unhealthy to Black minds. The white people of this generation cannot fix racism. This propaganda is the devil's work—and many of our own people have been fooled into spreading it.

Heed my words carefully. We do not need help, permission, or acceptance from white America to succeed. Our obsession with promulgating messages of white guilt is self-defeating and cancerous. A healthy relationship with positive social discourse among Black and white communities can begin only when we realize our power—and we work toward building one community.

It is no longer productive to have discussions about white fragility and white privilege. The conversation has been had. The focus on pain that white people and their ancestors have brought upon our people has been a focal point for decades...and decades...and decades. And though I will acknowledge that Black communities

BLACK RESILIENCE

have certainly made progress during this time period, we're not there yet.

We scream "Black Lives Matter" in the face of a white and privileged nation that enslaved our ancestors. White people scream back, "Yes, Black Lives Matter. We know and agree." This statement effectively spread awareness of racism; however, many good white Americans struggle to internalize their power to influence Black lives. Many good white Americans feel uncomfortable discussing racism. I can imagine that it might be difficult to have a discussion with Black people about matters they may not be cognizant of or about crimes and wrongs done by their ancestors—or more frequently, the ancestors of human beings who looked like them.

These discussions can be, and have been, important—and are often a necessary stage of grieving. But it is time for us to move beyond this and beyond our reliance on white guilt to free us from their racism.

Some of the loudest white allies have let their self-described "white privilege" get to their heads. Instead of making positive change in outcomes for Black people in impoverished communities, and like many sociopaths, many white allies have used the platform of racism to enrich themselves. Others who pose as "allies" pity us, believe we are inferior, and therefore view their participation in the Black Lives Matter movement as an act

217

of charity and evidence of their altruism. Are these truly allies? They sound pretty racist to me.

Since the very beginning of the Civil Rights Movement, the social discourse on racial issues have often been followed or preceded by acts of violence or legal action. Fighting. Always more fighting. Animosity breeding more animosity. But these are new times—calling for new solutions and ideologies about the Black condition and how to improve it. White-only meetings or initiatives about improving diversity will not improve Black quality of life, and neither will Black-only meetings or initiatives about banding together lifting each other up. Both of these scenarios represent progress from where we have come, but both reflect polarization—and a fractured America.

The problems we've examined in this book cannot be accomplished without white people pulling up the chair to the conversation. Life and success is a relationship game. How do you breach a predominantly white profession? How do you relate to your predominantly white colleagues? It cannot be achieved by having all-Black meetings—nor can it be accomplished by begging white people to stop being racist, give us a job, or be our friends. We need to make an effort to connect with our white brothers and sisters. We each need to have an open mind. We must cultivate a desire to develop and maintain relationships with those different from us and those whom we do not understand. We must not be afraid of integration. Polarization is Donald Trump's plan. The division of America is the devil's plan, and it's the enemy of progress. We have to find common ground. We have to find trust and forgiveness. We must build one community, one America.

Social scientists say the term *race* is a "social construct," that is, it was invented and given meaning by human beings. The creation of racial categories—white and Black—emerged early in our nation's history and was used to establish a racialized system of power and privilege. These categories were woven into national legal and political doctrine—leading to the institutionalization of racism. No nation in the world has institutionalized racism the way America has.

We have fought for years to remove systemic racism, as well as the legal and social prohibitions that plagued us. The final goals remain unconquered: equal educational opportunity and inclusion. Martin Luther King, Jr. was correct when he said, "Desegregation is enforceable...integration is not," because it requires us to work together to build one community. Integration is up to us, and it will require tact, skill, and empathy. Integration will require the proper strategy. Integration will require a clearly defined objective. Integration will require near-perfect execution. No one group of us, Black or white, can do this alone.

In order for this nation to heal, we must be clear in our demands for the resources and support with openness and respect. We should not need to rely on white allies to pave the way for Black success. Our nation is made up of thousands of different backgrounds, nationalities, races, religions, and ethnic groups. Our differences do not divide us so long as we don't see diversity as a disadvantage. In reality, the ethnic variety across the American population is part of what defines the country's greatness. It is time that we realize our destiny and hold our heads high. We are blessed, and we are chosen, and as such, we must focus on our own ability to create a positive change in our communities. Let's bridge the gaps, open the barriers that hold us hostage inside an echo chamber of our own making, and build meaningful connections without regard for race. Before pointing the finger outward, *we* must first look inwards to accept the value we have and the equality we inherently deserve. As imperfect human beings living in the modern world, we're all growing, learning, and adapting, which is something that should be encouraged to do as one. Whether you are brown, Black, or white—we're all in this together.

To this end, I have founded the Black Resilience Foundation, a 501(c)(3) nonprofit organization dedicated to the empowerment of Black communities through the message of BLACK RESILIENCE and the proliferation of positive ideas about Blackness.

The Black Lives Matter movement played an important role in raising awareness about the severe racism that plagues our country, but the Black community is now asking the urgent and imperative question: Where do we go from here?

Black Resilience has the answer.

It is the evolution and progression of #BlackLives Matter, carrying a voice that has been missing until now. It is a Black voice with a deeply rooted, practical perspective, a Black voice carrying more than the narratives of Black pain and Black problems, a Black voice that carries blueprints for solutions and strategies that will work today, despite the obstacles, despite white privilege, and yes, despite racism.

Through this foundation, we will secure funding commitments from corporations, banks, and philanthropies to advance our own goals and to support other new and existing Black-led organizations.

I believe passionately that Black ideas have created and will continue to create positive change in the world. This is why the Black Resilience Foundation is launching BxTalks. It will provide our community with a platform to spread positive ideas about Blackness.

BxTalks will enable our community to learn, share, and unify behind our common goal. We will welcome people from every discipline within our community to share their unique and specialized knowledge and ideas.

BxTalks will be dedicated to building a deep repository of collective wisdom and promote collaboration from the Black community's most inspired thinkers.

This is just the beginning. Together, I believe that we can spread awareness of the new movement, the Black Resilience Movement, spreading messages of Black enfranchisement and Black strength.